VIRGINIA NEW DRIVER'S GUIDE

THE BLESSED GUIDE TO PASSING THE LEARNER'S PERMIT TEST IN VIRGINIA MADE EASY

BLESSED DRIVING SCHOOL, LLC

WWW.BLESSEDDRIVINGSCHOOL.COM

ACKNOWLEDGMENTS

First and foremost, to God, my family, friends, students, and everyone who believed in me, thank you for your unwavering support and prayers. This book is a reflection of the love and guidance that surrounds me.

A special thanks goes to **Emma Kalka**, my steadfast writing partner, for her invaluable guidance and support throughout the writing process. Her insightful feedback, unwavering encouragement, and infectious enthusiasm were instrumental in shaping the narrative and bringing my vision to life. I am truly grateful for her collaboration.

I would also like to express my sincere gratitude to **Moses** from Fiverr for creating the beautiful and eye-catching book cover. His talent and attention to detail have greatly enhanced the overall presentation of this work.

Finally, I would like to acknowledge the assistance of **Publishing Services** in formatting the manuscript. Their professionalism and efficiency were instrumental in ensuring that the book was ready for publication.

TABLE OF CONTENTS

INTRODUCTION
MAY GOD BLESS YOU

There's nothing more frustrating than sitting down to take a test and then blanking out on the answers. Or maybe you've put in the hours studying, only to find you studied the wrong things. Perhaps you're one of those people who gets super anxious about tests even though you know the material, which translates into a bad score.

These are all very ordinary experiences. However, taking the learner's permit test can be even more frustrating. It's the first step in gaining more independence by becoming a licensed driver, so when you struggle to pass it, that defeat can be extra strong. Many may feel like we hit a brick wall when we cannot pass a test. King David said in 2 Samuel 22:30, "For by thee I have run through a troop: By my God have I leaped over a wall." So can you!

That's where we come in.

We're Blessed Driving School, LLC and here to teach everything you need to know so that you'll be relaxed and confident when you walk in to take your permit test. By the time you've finished this book and all the practice activities, you'll be able to pass your test with flying colors, no matter how you may have done in the past.

Almost everything we discuss in this book was taken from the Virginia DMV Driver's Manual and/or from our in-person Driver's Manual Re-Examination class. You will know how the test is formatted and administered, plus how to complete getting your driver's license. We'll also cover traffic laws and regulations and how to be a safe driver when you hit the roads.

You'll even learn how to safely operate and maintain a vehicle, as well as how to drive in special conditions such as rain or snow. Additionally, we'll teach you how to safely share the road with others, especially semis and RVs.

We'll even make sure that you can identify traffic signs in your sleep. Granted, we don't advise driving while you're sleepy. We want to make this a fun learning experience like our in-person classes!

You'll learn what to do in emergencies and every topic on which you will be quizzed when you take the test. Rest assured that we've covered those curveballs, so there won't be any. God willing, your confidence will increase as you learn everything required to pass the learner's permit test at the DMV on your first or next attempt.

Additionally, at the end of each chapter, you can take an online quiz to see how you're doing. To access these quizzes, you must first email your name, email address, and the last six digits of your UPC number to myclass@blesseddrivingschool.com. We'll set up your online account within 24 hours on the website:

www.blessedonlinedriversmanualcourse.com

Use this account to take the online quizzes.

You can breathe a little easier. Blessed Driving School is here to offer a helping hand and guide you on your journey to becoming a licensed driver. This book covers the first step, and we expect you to finish the work required to obtain your learner's permit. But we're also sure that we'll all have some fun along the way. So, let's get started.

CHAPTER 1

UNDERSTANDING THE
LEARNER'S PERMIT PROCESS

You are more than likely well aware of how difficult it can be to pass the Virginia DMV's learner's permit test. However, did you know that 25% to 30% of all first-time test takers don't pass? Some studies even say that only 30% of first-timers pass.

Either way, you're not alone. Many people struggle to pass the knowledge test on their first try. Luckily for you, Blessed Driving School is on your side, and we'll make sure that you are not only ready to take the test but can pass it.

Many of our students take either the online or in-person course we offer and pass the permit test on their first or second try. This means that you will have a much higher chance of getting the score you need just by studying this book. It's based on everything I teach in both classes, give or take a few fun anecdotes (don't worry—I'll try to include as many of those as I can).

All you need to do is take notes (specifically write down anything that is **bolded**) and pay attention. Not hard, right? If you still struggle with the test after studying this book, please take our class before attempting it again. And if you're unsure, just trust past students. As mentioned, many have reported that they passed the permit test on either the first or second attempt after our class.

That could be you.

Now, let's discuss the test, why you need to take it, and all the requirements involved. Then, I'll give you some tips and advice on studying and managing test anxiety before we dive into all the nitty-gritty details.

INTRODUCTION TO THE VIRGINIA DMV LEARNER'S PERMIT TEST

As you know, passing the Virginia DMV learner's permit test (also known as the knowledge test) is required to get a learner's permit and, eventually, a driver's license. Without passing this test, you can't move forward in the process, meaning there will be no cruising down the highway in your future - at least not in the driver's seat. Once you have passed the test, you'll be given a learner's permit and can move on to the next step - driving with a licensed driver who is at least 21 years old.

The knowledge test consists of two parts and tests your understanding of traffic signs, pavement markings, motor vehicle laws, and how to drive safely. It is a multiple-choice test administered on a computer. Part one consists of questions about road signs. To move on to the next part of the test, you must answer all of these questions correctly. Part two consists of general knowledge questions. You must correctly answer 80% of the questions to pass. DMV allows you three attempts at the learner's permit test before they require an 8-Hour Driver's Manual Re-Examination Course for the fourth attempt. Teens under 18 cannot take this 8-Hour course unless they have already completed Driver's Education.

Most of the information in this book is taken directly from the Virginia DMV Driver's Manual or our in-person Driver's Manual Re-Examination course. Past students have spoken to us about questions or answers they remember being on the test but not in the manual, so we've incorporated them into our lessons to help you have a better chance of passing the test. This is why taking notes is so important. With over 12 years of experience teaching people how to pass the knowledge test, you can trust us.

Not to mention, writing down notes will help you remember important information, which in turn will help you pass.

One of our previous students called us right after taking the permit test for the first time in complete shock. This student was an older woman who had been driving without a proper license for over 20 years and decided she wanted to take the steps to drive legally. After taking our course, she passed the test on her first try.

"Everything you said was on the test, and I passed," she exclaimed. "Everything you said was on the test!"

So, trust us. If we say you can pass this test, you can.

LEARNER'S PERMIT AND DRIVER'S LICENSE REQUIREMENTS

So, what exactly is a learner's permit? And how do you get one and then a driver's license? We've got you.

First of all, **whenever you drive, you must carry a valid driver's license or permit**. You cannot legally operate any kind of vehicle without one or the other, though there are extra requirements for a permit. Namely, there must be a licensed driver at least 21 years of age seated in the front passenger seat. Now please don't think you can drive with grandma Mable who is 120 years old because at that age she probably can't see real good and you got to be able to see if you want a driver's license.

If you are under 18, you must hold a learner's permit for nine months before obtaining a driver's license. If you are 18 or older, you must hold a learner's permit for 60 days OR present a driver's license education certificate of completion to apply for a driver's license.

Here is the breakdown of what you need to get a learner's permit.

- **Be at least 15 years and six months old.**
- **Complete a DL1M learner's permit and driver's license application form.**
- **Furnish proof of:**

  - **Identification, such as a social security card, state ID, passport or birth certificate**
  - **A social security number (you can simply write this down, and the DMV will digitally confirm it)**
  - **Residency**
  - **Legal presence**

- **Pass learner's permit test: signs (100%), general knowledge (80%).**
- **Vision test.**
- **Have a digitized photo taken at DMV.**

Please don't forget that last step. In our experience, we have seen a lot of ID's and the first thing many of our students tell us is, "Don't look at my picture, I won't ready." Trust us, many of them were not ready to take a picture. Ladies, please get your hair done before you go to the DMV. We want you looking cute. Guys, please go to the barber shop, shave, and slap on some cologne because now your lady doesn't have to drive you around everywhere, why? Because ladies and gentlemen, you are going to pass that test so you can legally drive with a licensed driver at least 21 years old. Please be ready to take a picture and don't forget to smile!

Now, once you get your learner's permit, you can stop there, or you can keep going and get a driver's license, which will allow you to drive a vehicle all on your own.

If you're ready to take on that kind of freedom (and responsibility), here's what you need.

Applicants 17 and under:

- **You must be at least 16 years and three months old.**
- **You must hold a learner's permit for at least nine months.**
- **You must successfully complete a driver education program.**
- **You must have parent/guardian permission.**
- **Your parents or guardians must certify that you have driven a motor vehicle for 45 hours, at least 10 of which were after sunset.**

Applicants 18 or older must hold a learner's permit for 60 days OR complete driver's education and behind the wheel lessons to get a 60-day waiver.

All Applicants:

- **You will need to complete a road test unless you hold a valid driver's license from another approved state or country.**

WHAT TO FOCUS ON DURING THE TEST

Okay, before all of your test anxiety starts building, stop. Take a deep breath and slowly let it out. Say a prayer or two for peace. Feel better? Now, before we get into all the details, here's an overview of what you can expect with the knowledge test.

The Virginia DMV permit test will cover important topics that any driver should know while on the road. You'll be tested on traffic signs (very important), right-of-way concepts, road markings, safe driving techniques, and traffic laws and regulations. We know this seems like a lot, but you need to know these things if you plan to be a safe driver.

Before you get overwhelmed by all the topics you'll need to study for the test, here are some tips from us at Blessed Driving School.

First of all—and we cannot say this enough, so it's not the last time you'll see this—write everything in this book that is **bolded** in your notes. Anything **bolded** will likely be on the test. Plus, the act of writing down notes will help cement the information in your memory.

Do not wait until the night before the test to cram everything into your memory. It didn't work in school, and it's not going to work with the permit test. All that will do is make you tired and even more anxious. Before you schedule your permit test, give yourself plenty of time to go through this book and study.

Also, don't think that you can pass with just a casual glance at the material. You really need to take a conscious, active look at the information in this book. Trust us. There is no terror like walking in to take the test after glancing at the book provided by the DMV - thinking you know all there is to know - only to discover that you can't remember anything. When that clock is ticking down and you only have a certain number of chances left, the anxiety is torture.

So, avoid all of that by studying with us. We'll make sure you know everything you need to know.

TESTING STRATEGIES

When the day arrives to take your permit test, we hope that after you study with our book, you'll be ready to take on the world. But just in case, here are some handy tips.

Be sure to get a good night's sleep. This actually worked in school, and it's the same now. A good night's sleep will leave you feeling rested and confident, plus it will help you retain information better. This is good not only the night before the test but also in the days leading up to your test.

Take your time studying. If you don't feel rushed, your anxiety levels will stay low, and you're less likely to forget answers or get them wrong.

Also, be mindful of the wording used in test questions. The DMV will try to trip you up. **If the question includes the word "always" or "never," the answer is usually false. This is because there is usually an exception to the rule.**

In the words of former U.S. Secretary of State Colin Powell, "There are no secrets to success. It is the result of preparation, hard work, and learning from failure." As long as you pay attention and put in the work, you will succeed in passing the permit test and be ready to move on to bigger things.

To see how you're doing, be sure to take the online quiz for this chapter at www.blessedonlinedriversmanualcourse.com to see how you're doing. If you still need to set up your account, just email your name, email address, and the last six digits of your ISBN number to myclass@blesseddrivingschool.com. We'll have your account ready for you in no time.

CHAPTER 2
VIRGINIA TRAFFIC LAWS AND REGULATIONS

W hen you're on the road, understanding traffic laws and signs can mean the difference between making it to that movie on time or ending up at the garage with a totaled car. Or worse - six feet under.

Here's a story for you.

There is a small town like pretty much any other small town. In this town, the city council installed new yield signs in a residential area to slow down speeders who cut through to avoid the traffic lights on the main road. Most drivers on this road understand what a yield sign means—to slow down and stop if there is cross traffic at the intersection.

Others, not so much. These drivers continued to speed down the road without slowing down or stopping at the intersections with yield signs. Each day, they barely avoided accidents until the local police department began patrolling and handing out citations. Only then did drivers start actually following the signs.

Understanding traffic laws is essential for passing the permit test and can also quite literally save you from a lot of grief. Trust us, you don't want to deal with that kind of rise in your insurance premiums.

OVERVIEW OF VIRGINIA TRAFFIC LAWS

Most traffic laws could be chalked up to common sense - don't speed, stop at stop signs and lights, and follow the right-of-way. However, there is a lot to remember. Additionally, there are situations when you're behind the wheel, and it could be confusing to know what to do. It's definitely not a good time to ask Jesus to take the wheel.

We're going to break down the most common traffic laws that you could encounter on the test so that you can not only understand them but also more easily commit them to memory. These laws might also just keep you out of an accident or ticket.

Common Traffic Laws and Regulations

Right-of-Way

Let's look at right-of-way concepts first. **Right-of-way is not a right or a privilege - it must be a given.** You must yield to traffic in specific situations to avoid accidents or tickets. **Additionally, yield also means to stop if you cannot merge safely into the flow of traffic.**

Let's examine four-way intersections. In general, if two vehicles from different directions arrive at an intersection at different times, it's first come, first served. **Whoever arrives first goes first.**

Now, let's get a bit trickier. When two or more cars coming from different directions arrive at the same time, remember this phrase: **Left is always last.** You must go last if you're making a left or on the left. This is the same if there are no signs or signals and if you're at an intersection where the traffic lights aren't working.

A good trick for answering questions like this on the test - when there are usually diagrams - is to picture yourself in the situation. See yourself sitting in your vehicle at the intersection. Look to your right. If there is a car, you don't go first - you have to wait for the person to your right to go. Then go clockwise. The driver without anyone on the right goes first, and then the next, and so on.

Another important place to yield is if you are entering an inter-state. **Drivers entering an interstate from an entrance ramp must yield the right-of-way to traffic already on the highway.** Other drivers may pull into the left lane to let you safely merge, but it's not their obligation. Also, drivers entering any intersection or traffic circle must yield to traffic already in it.

Now, let's say you're driving down the road, and you come up to a school bus. **All traffic must stop for a school bus with flashing red lights and an extended stop sign UNLESS the vehicles are traveling on the opposite side of a highway with a physical barrier or unpaved median area.** You must also stop if the bus is loading or unloading children and the signal devices are not functioning properly. **Only move when the bus moves and the way is clear.** You cannot forget about those babies. If the bus is moving on, but you still have children crossing the street, you need to stay put until they are safely on the other side.

Emergency vehicles are other vehicles with flashing lights that you need to look out for. If you see flashing lights, it's important not to freak out —there are specific actions you must take when you see them, be they blue, red, yellow, or white. **First of all, never follow an emergency vehicle closer than 500 feet when its lights are**

flashing. Let's be honest: most of the time, they move fairly quickly, and you shouldn't be speeding anyway.

If police, fire, or rescue vehicles approach you from behind using a siren, flashing lights, or both, you must immediately yield the right-of-way. Safely pull over to the right edge of the road and stop until the emergency vehicle has passed. What if they are coming from the other direction? You only need to pull over if you are on a road or highway that isn't divided.

That means if you're on the interstate and an ambulance comes from the opposite side of the road and there's a barrier or median, you can keep going. If there's not, safely pull over to the right and remain stopped until they pass.

Next, let's say you're driving to the grocery store and suddenly come across a funeral procession or a military convoy. What do you do?

You must yield to funeral processions. Don't cut through. Don't join them so that you can get to Walmart down the road faster. Don't interfere. You'll be able to know who is in the procession as they will be driving slowly and usually have their hazard lights on. Also, unless there is a police escort, the lead car in a procession must follow all traffic laws.

You also don't want to mess with military convoys. Always yield and never cut through or join. This isn't a War of the Worlds situation. You don't need to get in line with them. Military vehicles are made of steel; if there is an accident, they will crush you.

We have a question for you: Do pedestrians always have the right-of-way?

Think about it, and write down your answer.

If you wrote yes, then you're wrong. (Remember what we said about "always" or "never"?) As a driver, there are two places where you yield to pedestrians. **You must yield for pedestrians who are crossing a street within a clearly marked crosswalk or at an unmarked intersection.** Also, remember that turning on red is especially hazardous for pedestrians. Avoid conflict and let them cross the street safely.

This isn't to say it's open season on pedestrians in other situations. If you're going down the interstate and someone makes a flying leap across it, you should still try to stop or avoid them if you can safely. While you don't want to hit the runner, you also don't want to put yourself or other drivers into an even more dangerous situation.

Also, if you are entering a street from a private road or driveway, you must stop and yield to all traffic and pedestrians.

Pavement Markings

Any driver who hits the road must know what those lines and colors mean. They aren't just there for decoration; they have important information.

First, look at the yellow lines. **Solid yellow center lines indicate two-way traffic, and when passing is allowed.** You must always stay to the right of the line. We're not in Britain or Japan.

Quiz time! You should never cross a double solid line - true or false? Go ahead and write down your answer.

If you wrote false, then you're starting to catch on. Again, those pesky always or never questions. **Crossing double yellow lines is permitted when you are making a left turn.**

If you see broken yellow lines, passing is permitted in either direction. You should pass only when the way ahead is clear. Also, you should not speed while passing. Think of it this way - if your grandma is driving in front of you and going 20 miles below the speed limit, you can pass. If it's someone who is going just a few miles under and you're being impatient, don't pass. You should also ensure that the line in front of the car you're passing isn't solid before moving into the other lane.

Now, if you have a yellow line that is broken on one side and solid on the other, **passing is permitted on the broken line side.** If you're on the solid side - don't pass. You'll also sometimes see one solid yellow line on the left edge of a road. This marks the left edge of the road when on a divided highway or a one-way street.

Okay, now let's take a look at white lines on a road. **White lines separate lanes of traffic going in the same direction. They also indicate one-way traffic.** Be careful about test questions regarding white lines. They will try to trip you up by thinking they indicate passing is permitted. White lines are not about passing - they indicate one-way traffic. Remember that.

If you see broken white lines, it means **drivers may cross them with caution. Solid white lines designate turn lanes and prevent lane changes near intersections.** Let's say you're coming to an intersection, and as you go through it, you see a Wawa on your right. Of course, you want to pop in to get a coffee or quesadilla. However, if you're in the left lane, DO NOT SWITCH TO THE RIGHT LANE. There's usually another entrance, or you can go down and turn around. Wait until you are safely through the intersection before you change lanes.

Arrows indicate which turns may be made from the lane. If you see a curved arrow and the word "only," this means you can only turn in the direction the arrow indicates. If you see a curved and straight arrow, this means you can either turn in the direction of the arrow or keep going straight.

Stop lines, crosswalks, and parking spaces are also marked by white lines. Solid white lines mark the right edge of the pavement.

Speed Limits

This next part should be a given, but we here at Blessed Driving School know there are a lot of speed demons out there. Plus, there might be some regulations that surprise you. Before we get into that, we'll get the obvious out of the way. What is a speed limit? A speed limit is the maximum legal speed at which you can travel on a road under ideal conditions - ideal conditions are super important to remember. You can drive slower than the posted speed, but it is illegal to drive faster. By law, you must drive slower if conditions make the posted speed unsafe. For example, you don't want to keep going 70 on the interstate if it's pouring down rain or there's road construction. Slow down.

These are the maximum speed limits for passenger vehicles and motorcycles unless posted otherwise:

- **Interstate Highways in Certain Rural Areas: 70 MPH**
- **Non-rural Interstate Highways, Public Roads Not Part of the Interstate System: 55 MPH**
- **Rural Rustic Roads: 35 MPH**
- **School, Business, and Residential Zones: 25 MPH**

* You are required to travel 25 MPH in a school zone only when indicated by a sign or signal. Otherwise, maintain the posted speed.

Understanding Road Signs and Signals

Road signs can be confusing simply because there are so many of them. However, there are the most common ones that just about everyone understands. If you see a red octagon, you know to stop. If you see a yellow sign with two people walking between lines, that means a crosswalk is coming up. Those white rectangles with a number on them - speed limit.

Here is a real-life example.

Let's say you come to an intersection that has an upside-down triangle outlined in red with "Yield" in the middle. What do you do? Do you slow down? Stop completely? Look both ways and continue. Ignore them?

If you ignored them completely, well, sorry to say that you could be getting a ticket if there's a traffic officer around. (And an incorrect answer on the knowledge test.) Yield signs are meant to be treated similarly to stop signs. If you come to an intersection with a yield sign, slow down first. Come to a stop if you need to. Next, check for cross traffic. If there is none, you can go through the intersection. However, if you see another vehicle coming, you must remain stopped until they have passed and the way is clear.

If you go through an intersection with a yield sign and hit cross-traffic, you'll be found in the wrong.

Let's break this down further. The first thing to know about road signs and signals is that the colors have meanings. They are a quick and easy way to let you, the driver, know what's coming up. Rather than killing yourself to memorize all the different signs that are out there - trust us, it's a lot - study what the colors and shapes mean. This can help give you a hint if you need to remember what a specific sign means. Passing the test at the DMV can be about more than just knowing the right answer but being able to eliminate the wrong ones.

Here's what you need to know.

Red	Prohibitive or Stop
Blue	Motorist Services Signs
Green	Guide Information, such as Directions or Guidance Signs
Yellow	General Warning
Orange	Construction and Maintenance Work
White	Regulatory Signs
Pink	Hazardous Materials (HAZMAT)
Brown	Recreational and Cultural Interest
Fluorescent Optic Yellow	School Zones, School Crossings, and Pedestrian Crossings

The next thing you need to understand is that the shapes also have meaning. This is what you can glean from them.

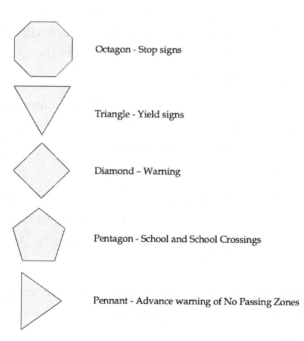

Octagon - Stop signs

Triangle - Yield signs

Diamond – Warning

Pentagon - School and School Crossings

Pennant - Advance warning of No Passing Zones

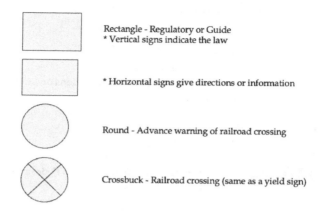

Rectangle - Regulatory or Guide
* Vertical signs indicate the law

* Horizontal signs give directions or information

Round - Advance warning of railroad crossing

Crossbuck - Railroad crossing (same as a yield sign)

Types of Signs

Warning Signs: These give advanced warnings of hazards to allow drivers time to minimize risks safely. Examples include winding roads, crosswalks, merging, lanes ending, roads that are slippery when wet, detours, and road work.

Guide Signs: These guide drivers to their destination by identifying routes well in advance. Examples include letting you know upcoming exits, mile markers, upcoming intersections, which way to merge, and more.

Information Signs: These inform drivers of motorist services and recreational facilities and include highway signs, rest stop notifications, upcoming restaurants and hotels, upcoming gas stations, and so on.

Regulatory Signs: These regulate the speed and movement of traffic. They include one-way signs, stop signs, speed limit signs, yield signs, and so on.

Traffic Violations and Penalties

What are the most common traffic violations? It will probably come as no surprise that the most common traffic violation in Virginia is speeding. Whether you're auditioning to be a stunt driver or just running late, lots of people speed. However, you can also get a speeding ticket for going the speed limit. Remember that "ideal conditions" thing? If you hit a freak snowstorm, a tornado, or there's smoke on the highway - or any situation where there is low visibility - and you're still going 65 MPH, you could get pulled over and receive a speeding citation.

Other common violations include failure to yield (cutting off those with the right-of-way), following too closely to the car in front of you, passing when it's unsafe, and failing to stop for pedestrians.

If you commit a traffic violation, you'll usually receive a citation (a ticket) with a fine. The specifics depend on the violation.

While you don't need to memorize the fine amounts for the test, they are important to know in general. Here are some examples.

For speeding, this will typically cost you $6 for every mile over the speed limit you were driving on the highway, $7 per mile over the speed limit in a school or work zone, and $8 per mile over the speed limit plus $200 in a residential area. You'll also need to pay a processing fee of $66 to $86.

Now, if you like to pretend you're the main character in "The Fast and The Furious," you'll probably face some harsher penalties. You could face a reckless driving charge if you're pulled over for going 20 MPH over the posted speed limit. This is a Class 1 misdemeanor for your first offense and comes with a hefty minimum $250 fine, a max of $2,500, and 12 months in jail. A second offense could be deemed a felony.

On the flip side, there is such a thing as driving too slow. If you are found impeding traffic by going too slow, you could be fined $30 plus the processing fee of $66.

For failure to yield, you could face up to 12 months in jail, up to $2,500 in fines, and a driver's license suspension of 10 days up to six months. Most of the time, you'll get off with just a citation and fine, but it's better to be safe than sorry.

Another thing you need to know is that Virginia has a points system. In addition to paying fines and facing potential court with traffic violations, you will also receive demerit points that could affect your license. The DMV monitors your driving record to see how many demerit points you receive in a 12-month and 24-month period.

Each violation adds a specific number of demerit points to your driving record. Typically, this ranges from three to six points and stays on your record for two to 11 years. Generally, you'll receive three points for speeding (1-9 MPH over), improper U-turn, improper passing, and driving without a valid license. You'll get four points for reckless driving, unsafe passing, following too closely, and improper signals. And finally, you'll get a whopping six demerit points for speeding in excess of 80 MPH, road racing, DUI, manslaughter, and driving with a suspended license.

You can offset these demerit points by earning safe driver points. This can be done by taking a driver improvement course (like the one we offer at Blessed Driving School) or going through an entire calendar year without receiving any moving violations or license suspensions.

It's important to be aware at all times so that you don't commit any traffic violations. Yes, we all have those days when we're tired or in a rush, but you never know when a traffic officer is lurking. Not to mention, you could prevent an accident.

It's story time again.

Once upon a time, there was a driver headed to a shopping center. They were turning right into the parking lot at an intersection with a red light - which is generally accepted unless posted. The driver looked to the left and didn't see any oncoming traffic, so they started turning in. However, they failed to notice that the traffic signals indicated a left turn was allowed for the center turning lanes. Thankfully, they saw this at the last second and stopped, leaving plenty of room for another vehicle to safely make a left turn into the parking lot and avoid an accident.

Unfortunately, that vehicle was a police officer.

The driver pulled in and parked. The officer pulled up next to them and issued a ticket for $150. Unfortunately, the driver had also recently moved to the area from another state and was just outside of the allowed time period to get a new license and plates. Luckily, the police officer was understanding and only issued a warning for that violation.

Moral of the story: Always pay attention to traffic laws and regulations.

ALCOHOL REGULATIONS AND IMPAIRED DRIVING LAWS

Overview of Alcohol Regulations

Most people know that it's illegal to drink and drive. We've all seen "drink responsibly" during alcohol commercials and know that bartenders can and will cut you off if they feel you've had too much. However, it's important to know and understand the alcohol regulations whether or not you plan to get behind the wheel. Plus, it's likely to be on the knowledge test.

Legally, drivers 21 or older are considered to be driving under the influence (DUI) if their blood alcohol content (BAC) is .08 percent or higher. If your driving is impaired, you can be convicted of driving under the influence with a BAC lower than .08 percent. Additionally, if under the age of 21, you can be convicted of illegal consumption of alcohol if your BAC is at least .02 percent but less than .08 percent.

Okay. We hear you. What on earth is blood alcohol content? How many drinks is .08 percent?

In short, BAC is the measure of the percentage of alcohol in a person's bloodstream.

How many drinks get you to .08 percent varies from person to person. Everyone metabolizes alcohol differently. It depends on your biological sex, weight, what you're drinking, and how long it's been since you've had that drink.

For example, a woman weighing 150 pounds will (generally) have a BAC of .02 percent an hour after drinking one beer. If that same woman has three beers within two hours, she'll hit .09 percent BAC, which is over the limit. However, a man weighing 200 pounds and drinking the same amount of beer in the same amount of time will have a BAC of .05%.

It should be noted that **12 ounces of beer (usually one can) is the same as a shot of liquor or a five-ounce glass of wine.**

If you are arrested for drinking and driving, the penalties are severe. If police have probable cause to pull you over and suspect that you've been drinking or using drugs, they will ask you to take a breath or blood test. It is important to know that under implied consent laws, you agree to take a test upon request if you're pulled over on a public road in Virginia.

If you're involved in a crash and it's believed that you are under the influence - and there is probable cause - police can arrest you for DUI within three hours of the crash without a warrant and at any location.

If you refuse to take a breath test or have a BAC of .08 percent or higher while driving, you can be charged with a DUI. Your driving privilege will be automatically suspended. The time range depends on the offense:

- First offense - 7 days
- Second offense - 60 days or until you go to trial, whichever comes first
- Third offense or more - until the trial

If convicted of DUI, the court and DMV will impose a suspension/revocation and other penalties in addition to the administrative license suspension. If you receive multiple DUI convictions, the periods will run consecutively.

What is the difference between having your license suspended or revoked?

If your license is suspended, your privilege to drive has been withdrawn temporarily. You may pay the required fees and reinstate your license at the end of the suspension period. You will also be required to show proof of legal presence - that you're a U.S. citizen or legally authorized by the federal government to be in the country. If your license has expired one year or more during the suspension period, you need to show proof of legal presence and pass the two-part knowledge, road skills, and vision exams to get your license back.

Revocation means your privilege to drive has been terminated. In order to get it back, you have to apply for a new license and show proof of legal presence once the revocation period has ended. This includes the vision test, two-part knowledge exam, and road skills test.

The court will revoke or suspend your license if you are convicted of the following:

- Operating a motor vehicle while under the influence of alcohol or drugs.
- Injuring another person as a result of operating a motor vehicle while under the influence of alcohol or drugs.
- Operating a motor vehicle while under suspension or revocation for a DUI.
- Operating a motor vehicle that is not equipped with the ignition interlock device when it is required by the court or DMV.
- Making a false statement to the DMV.
- Failing to stop and identify yourself at the scene of a crash if someone has been injured or killed.
- Voluntary or involuntary manslaughter resulting from driving a motor vehicle.
- Involuntary manslaughter resulting from operating a motor vehicle while under the influence of alcohol.
- Committing a drug offense, regardless of whether or not a motor vehicle was involved.
- Committing a felony involving the use of a motor vehicle.

- Taking a driver's license exam for another person or appearing for another person to renew a license.
- Eluding police.

The best solution if you plan to go out and drink is to not get behind the wheel. Designate someone in your group to remain sober and drive everyone home at night's end. You can also figure out how much time is needed for you to sober up and stop drinking before you need to leave. Let's take the lady we spoke about earlier. If she drinks two beers in two hours, her BAC will be .05 percent. It'll take about three hours for her BAC to get back down to 0 percent. While they are not 100 percent accurate - and should not be taken as gospel - there are BAC calculators you can find online to help you figure this out.

It is important to know that the only thing that can get alcohol out of your system is time.

Regardless of whether you will drive (and we HIGHLY recommend that you don't), always drink responsibly.

Impaired Driving Consequences and Prevention

Driving while impaired is dangerous for you and everyone on the road with you. And yes, even if you're not a heavy drinker, you can still face the consequences of drinking and driving. Nearly 50 percent of drivers arrested for DUI are social to moderate drinkers. So, definitely don't think that it won't happen to you.

Just one alcoholic drink can affect your driving ability. Common side effects include elevated confidence, blurred vision, memory loss, slower reaction time, fatigue, and sickness. Driving errors occur when you're overconfident. **Your chances of being in a crash are seven times greater if you drive after drinking than**

if you drive sober. According to researchers, **three out of every ten drivers are drunk between the hours of 10 p.m. and 2 a.m.**

Several students here at Blessed Driving School have reported that getting a DUI cost them over $10,000. You have to consider lost time from work, paying for every day your car is impounded, legal fees, classes like the driver improvement course, and an interlock device that must be put on the vehicle to allow it to start.

Outside of the penalties, driving drunk could very likely result in a car accident. Too often, we read about drunk driving accidents in the news that result in the death of one or both drivers. That one drink could lead to you unintentionally ending your own life or that of someone else.

As mentioned, the best way to avoid this is not to drink and drive. Most cities have rideshare services, making it easier to go out, have a few drinks, and still get home safely without getting behind the wheel. Again, you can also use a designated driver. If you're drinking at a friend's house, maybe plan to stay there for the night. Or at least until you are completely sober and can safely drive.

AUTO INSURANCE REQUIREMENTS

Understanding Auto Insurance Laws

I'm sure as soon as someone mentions the word "insurance," you're all ready to check out of the conversation. Yes, it can be boring. It can most definitely be confusing. But if you plan to drive, it is a requirement to own a car. To register a vehicle and obtain a driver's license, **you must have liability insurance or pay the $500 uninsured motor vehicle fee.**

There are three main kinds of insurance - liability, collision, and comprehensive. Liability insurance is money you owe someone for something you did to them or their property. If you're involved in a crash with another vehicle, usually - unless you drive a Cadillac from the 80s that's built like a tank - you will damage your car and their car. Collision insurance covers the person's car that's at fault. Your lender will require collision insurance - not the DMV. Finally, comprehensive coverage covers anything that isn't considered a crash. This could be a rock hitting your windshield or hitting someone else's car with your door while getting out of your car at Walmart.

When you get a car, you must insure it with a company authorized to do business in Virginia. **There are also some minimum requirements for liability insurance:**

- **$30,000 for injury or death of one person**
- **$60,000 for injury or death of two or more people**
- **$20,000 for property damage.**

In addition, insurance companies may factor in the driving records of any individual of driving age who resides within an insured person's household when figuring the policy premium. We definitely recommend talking to your company if you have any questions about the impact a newly licensed driver will have on your policy.

Choosing the right policy comes down to what you want. Obviously, you have to meet the liability requirements, but often, insurance companies will include extras like roadside assistance if your car breaks down or you get a flat. This will raise your premiums; however, it could save you money and stress in the event that you're stuck in the left turn lane because your battery suddenly shuts off. (Trust us—it's not fun, but it's much easier to handle with roadside assistance.)

Take the time to compare policies with several different companies before settling on one. And really look into the details of what is included before going with the lowest price.

Importance of Auto Insurance and Financial Responsibility

Obviously, auto insurance definitely comes in handy for those accidents. Whether you're driving while tired and accidentally rear-ended someone or come back from shopping to find a dent in your car, it can help alleviate the cost of fixing the damage, depending on the situation.

Imagine you're driving to work. You're alert. Everything is going smoothly. You're following traffic laws and, in general, being a safe driver. Maybe Kirk Franklin is on Spotify, and you're bopping along with it. You come to an intersection and stop at a stop sign. It's your turn to go, but someone else is running late and decides to run it. They t-bone your car.

If you're not at fault, the other person's insurance will pay for the repairs. Some policies also cover the cost of a rental car while yours is in the shop getting fixed.

It's important not only to get auto insurance but also to maintain it.

Getting behind on your payments could cause your insurance to lapse, and the same could happen if you forget to renew your policy. Drivers must also keep proof of insurance in their vehicle at all times. Failure to comply with insurance regulations could have your driver's license revoked or suspended. To be reinstated, you'll have to pay a $600 statutory fee, file a Financial Responsibility Insurance Certificate with the DMV for three years, and pay a reinstatement fee, if applicable.

So, make life easier and more stress-free for yourself. Keep up with your auto insurance.

To see how you're doing, be sure to take the online quiz for this chapter at www.blessedonlinedriversmanualcourse.com to see how you're doing. If you still need to set up your account, just email your name, email address, and the last six digits of your ISBN number to myclass@blesseddrivingschool.com. We'll have your account ready for you in no time.

CHAPTER 3
SAFE DRIVING PRACTICES

What should you do before you drive off for the day?

Go ahead, take a guess. Write it down if you want.

If you said put on a seatbelt, then you would be right. It is just one of many things that you should do before taking off in your car. The very first step is to walk around the vehicle, check the ground for leaks, and look at the tires to see if the pressure is low (do this at least once a day). When you get inside, you should make all your adjustments before you buckle up - adjust your seat, mirrors, hair, temperature, radio, put your phone away, and so on. Then you can put your seatbelt on.

We all know you should buckle up whether you're a driver or a passenger. It can save you from serious harm or even death in an accident. In 2021, 26,325 passenger vehicle occupants were killed, with 50% of those not wearing any seat belts, according to the

National Highway Traffic Safety Administration. Thankfully, seat belt use is rising, hitting 91.9% in 2023.

If you buckle up in the front seat, you can reduce the risk of fatal injury by 45 percent and moderate to critical injury by 50%, also according to the NHTSA.

Seat belts and airbags are just two parts of safe driving that could be on the knowledge test. Let's take a deeper look.

DEFENSIVE DRIVING TECHNIQUES

Overview of Defensive Driving Principles

So, what is defensive driving? Essentially, it's driving in a way that uses safe strategies to help you address potential hazards on the road. These strategies include safely navigating heavy rain or following at a safe distance to avoid accidents. You will likely see a few questions about safe driving on the test.

Searching/Scanning

Searching or scanning means looking at the entire scene for anything that might come into your path. You should keep your eyes moving and avoid staring at one thing. It's essential to learn to read the road and your surroundings.

Looking ahead can help you spot risks early and give you more time to react. **Expert drivers try to focus their eyes 20 to 30 seconds ahead.** If you're driving in a city, this is about one block ahead. You'll want to avoid staring at the middle of the road. Scan side to side, noting all the traffic signs and signals, cars, people, and anything that could be on the road by the time you reach them.

You'll also want to play a bit of Nancy Drew. **Search for clues on the road.** Check for exhaust smoke, brake or back-up lights, and turned wheels on vehicles. This tells you that a car might be about to pull into your path. Be aware of pedestrians or cyclists - they could potentially cross your path ahead as well.

Let's say you're driving in a rural area - watch for hidden intersections and driveways, curves, hills, and different road conditions. We can tell you this: sometimes you don't know what you'll see out in the country. It could be normal and quiet, or you might get cows in the road (or in the air if it's a twister sort of day). You'll also want to keep an eye out for other vehicles, especially trucks, oversized and slow-moving farm vehicles, and bicycles.

Check from left to right and then left again before entering an intersection. Any time you come to a place on the road where other cars, people, or animals may cross your path, look both ways to be sure it's clear. You look left first because anything coming from that direction is closer to you.

Here's where you should definitely be scanning:

- Intersections
- Crosswalks
- Shopping centers
- Construction areas
- Playgrounds

Look behind you. Use your rearview mirror to check the traffic behind you frequently, about every 10 seconds. You'll know if someone is coming up behind you too quickly or tailgating. You'll also need to check your mirror when changing lanes, backing up, slowing down quickly, or driving down a long, steep hill.

Visibility

As we've stated before, most of what you do while driving depends on what you see. To be a good driver, you need to know what to look for, where to look, and how to adjust to any possible problems. **The single biggest contributor to crashes is failing to identify a risk.** Look at the road, look to the sides, and look behind you. Be ready for unexpected events. Also, use your headlights at night and whenever it's hard to see.

Virginia law requires that you use headlights when visibility is reduced to 500 feet in inclement weather, such as rain, fog, snow, or sleet. Also, you have to use your headlights when you use your windshield wipers as a result of bad weather.

At sunset, turn on your headlights as soon as the light begins to fade to make your vehicle more visible to others. Headlights must be used from sunset to sunrise. If driving in towns or cities, you must use your low beams unless you're on a street with no light. Always switch to low beams when you meet oncoming traffic.

Write this down. **No high beams within 200 feet following and 500 feet approaching.**

If the high beams of an oncoming car are on, don't look at them directly. Glance to the side of the road and look quickly ahead to determine the other vehicle's position. Keep doing this until you pass them. Even if they don't dim their headlights, do not flash them with your high beams.

There are important things to know about headlights and fog, but we'll get into those just a little bit later on in this chapter.

Space Management

Allowing enough space around your car while driving gives you the distance to react if there is an emergency. Create a space cushion by staying in the middle of your lane and making sure there is enough room ahead of and behind your vehicle. That way, other vehicles can pass or stop safely. Think of it as a personal space bubble for your car. No one likes someone with garlic breath hanging out too close to their nose, just as they don't like another car riding their tail.

Definitely write this down. **Use the two-, three- and four-second rule to determine if you are following far enough behind the vehicle ahead of you.** "How do I do this?" you may ask. Well, it's pretty simple. When the car in front of you passes a stationary object, count out how many seconds until you pass it. Depending on the speed you're driving, you should count to two, three, or four seconds before your car reaches the same stationary object.

At these posted speeds and on dry surfaces, this distance, in seconds, allows the driver to steer and brake out of problem areas:

- **2 seconds Under 35 MPH**
- **3 seconds 36-45 MPH**
- **4 seconds 46-70 MPH**

Notice - there is no safe following distance for 100 MPH so please don't even think about going that fast unless you are on a race track.

You must change the following distance when the speed or road conditions change. Hand response time is close to half a second, and foot response time is three-quarters of a second. However, this doesn't consider any delay in perception time caused by a driver being tired, on medication, distracted, or other factors. Additionally, road conditions, speed, driver alertness, and even following vehicles of different weights change the ability to stop.

Increase your following distance when driving:

- **behind a large vehicle that blocks your vision**
- **in bad weather or heavy traffic**
- **when exiting an expressway**
- **behind a motorcycle**
- **when being tailgated**

Lane Changes

Before changing lanes, check your side and rearview mirrors for traffic approaching you from behind. Then, use your turn signal to let other drivers know you plan to change lanes. Check for other drivers who also may be moving into the same lane. Before moving into the other lane, quickly glance over your shoulder and check for any vehicles in your blind spot.

Whether changing lanes, passing, entering or exiting a highway, always use your turn signals and check traffic to the rear and sides. When driving on a multi-lane highway, stay in the right lane if you drive slower than the traffic around you.

Passing

When passing another vehicle, you should check the traffic ahead, behind you, and in your blind spot before you attempt to pass. Signal and then accelerate. **Return to the right lane after you are able to see the entire front of the passed vehicle in your rearview mirror. It is against the law to exceed the speed limit as you pass.**

Complete the pass before you reach a no-passing zone. If you're still in the left lane when you reach it, you're breaking the law. You can pass on the right if the vehicle you're passing has signaled and is turning left. You need to be careful, though. The vehicle could be blocking your view or the view of other drivers.

Don't pass on the right if you need to drive off the pavement or the main portion of the roadway to get around the other vehicle.

If you're approaching or passing a person on a bike, moped, power-assisted bicycle or other device, reduce your speed and pass at least three feet to the left.

When being passed, don't speed up. Maintain a steady speed or slow down.

Here are times when passing is unlawful and unsafe:

- On hills, curves, at intersections, or railroad crossings, except on roads with two or more lanes of traffic moving in the same direction
- Off the pavement or shoulder of the road
- When a school bus is stopped to load or unload passengers on a public road (unless a physical barrier or unpaved median separates traffic going in either direction) or on a private road
- When a solid line marks the left side of your lane

Roundabouts

Roundabouts are other road areas where you need to watch your surroundings and follow the rules. Otherwise, you might end up getting into an accident or driving around in circles all day. Neither sounds like fun.

Here are tips for driving safely through a roundabout.

As you come up to a roundabout, look for the street and direction signs. These will help you know what exit you need to take. They are generally posted along the roadside before you get to the roundabout. When you get to it, yield the right-of-way to pedestrians and bicyclists. **You also need to yield to any vehicles already in the roundabout.** The entry point will sometimes be controlled by a stop or yield sign or even a traffic signal. When the way is clear, you can enter.

Once you get inside the roundabout, stay in your lane until you're ready to exit. Use the right-turn signal to let drivers around you know what you plan to do. **Don't change lanes or take an exit before checking for vehicles that may be continuing through the roundabout in the lane next to you or behind you.** You should expect vehicles to be in blind spots you can't see in your rearview or side view mirrors. Glance over your shoulder to check for any vehicles in those spots.

Over-correcting

What is over-correcting? This is when the driver turns the steering wheel more sharply than expected, causing the rear wheels to slide toward the outside of the turn. It could result in losing control and potentially lead to a crash. **Most over-correction crashes are single-vehicle crashes and are usually preventable.**

This is why it's so important to remain alert at all times. If you're on a curved road, reduce your speed and use extra caution. If there are a lot of cars around you, also slow down and be more aware. If you veer off the road - whether it's curved or straight - don't lose it or panic. Just gradually reduce your speed, look in the direction you want to go, and slowly steer back on the road.

Mirror Settings and BGE

Here is another thing that you should write down - **BGE, Blind spot Glare Elimination. Adjusting the side mirror setting 15 degrees outward lets you see the lanes to the sides and doesn't overlap too much with the area you can already see in your rearview mirror.**

Set your rearview mirror to see 200 feet behind you and your side mirrors 15 degrees out to see the adjacent lanes. There are more blind spots when you tilt your mirrors in. When you tilt your mirrors out, by the time a car that is passing you reaches close enough that you could open your door and hit them, they will be in your peripheral vision. This means you can see them without turning your head.

How do you set your mirrors the right way? Lean in until your head is almost touching the window on the driver's side (though don't touch it because if your hair is greasy, you don't want that on the window) tilt the mirror out until you can almost see the back corner of your car, but you can't see it when you're straight. For the other mirror, lean to the right and do the same. Set it where you can almost see the back corner on the opposite side when you lean, but not when sitting straight.

Let's look at some scenarios.

Imagine you're driving down a two-lane highway. There are few other cars on the road. But rather than let your mind wander, you keep alert and watch the pastures on both sides.

Out of the corner of your eye, you see something streaking towards the road. You gradually slow down, even though there's still a decent amount of space and time before you reach whatever it is.

Out of the brush, a large dog bounds towards the road. You keep your cool. You don't veer over into the left lane. You keep reducing your speed and are prepared to stop. Thankfully, the dog spins around and bounces back into the pasture. You avoid hitting it, and the car now passing you from the other direction.

Defensive and safe driving is about being alert. It would be best if you constantly were scanning your surroundings so you can see any potential dangers and give yourself enough time to react safely.

Now, let's say you're on a multi-lane interstate with cars all around you. You come up to an SUV following a semi. Sensing you could be stuck there until it's safe to pass, you slow down and give yourself plenty of space. You constantly check your mirrors, waiting for an opening to pass. Once you think the way is clear, you check your blind spot and notice a car is there.

While you wait in your lane for the car to pass, the SUV in front of you does not. To avoid hitting the car, they veer back into the lane. However, you've stayed far enough behind to slow down and avoid accidents safely. Once the way is clear, you signal and move into the left lane, passing the SUV and semi.

Be alert. Give yourself space. If a situation looks like it could be unsafe, slow down and make sure you are at a safe distance to avoid an accident. This includes stopping if you need to and it's safe to do so.

Handling Adverse Driving Conditions

Now that we've covered safe driving techniques during the best of conditions, we're going to take a look at driving when Mother Nature decides to be temperamental.

Fog is a very common weather condition that you can face on the road. It is most common during the fall and winter and forms overnight as the air near the ground cools. It starts close to the ground and thickens as the air continues to cool.

An important note for driving through fog - it reflects light and can reflect your own headlights back into you. **This is why you should use low-beam headlights in heavy fog and look for the road edge markings to guide you.** They will help you know when you're coming to the road's edge or veering into the next lane. A light fog will still reduce visibility and your ability to judge distances, so SLOW DOWN.

Driving in heavy rain can be just as hazardous as driving in fog, especially if there's wind. It's especially difficult to see other vehicles behind you and in blind spot areas. Again, use your low-beam headlights. Turn your windshield wipers on if it's light rain or drizzle, but avoid doing this if it's sprinkling. It could smear the rain and make it harder to see. Make sure you have windshield wiper fluid in that case. **Also, according to Virginia law, if your wipers are on, so should your headlights.** You must know this for the test.

It's important to know that the roads are the most slippery during the first half-hour of rain. This is because the water mixes with the oil on the street. Be very careful driving through pooled water—it can cause you to hydroplane or lose control.

When it snows, be sure to remove all snow and ice from your car before you start driving. This includes the roof, hood and rear of the vehicle. If you leave this on your car, it could fly off while you're in motion and create a hazard for other cars. You'll also want to clear all your windows, mirrors and front and rear lights so you can see and communicate with other drivers.

As we're sure you know, driving on snow or ice is slippery. If you live in an area that gets a lot of snow, it's a good idea to use all-weather snow tires or chains to help you keep the best grip. It will help prevent skidding and reduce your stop time. When you brake, apply the brakes gently. Slow down before stopping or turning.

Here's a trick for stopping on snow or ice: release the accelerator and apply the brakes gently. You have the most traction when the front tires are rolling. Rather than hard braking, keep a slow and steady speed so you can better control your vehicle.

Also, be sure to watch for ice on bridges and in shady areas. Bridges tend to freeze before other road surfaces.

One of the scariest experiences I've had is driving on an interstate —surrounded by semis and other cars—when a freak rainstorm hits. One second, everything is fine; the next, torrential rain falls, and visibility is now random splotches of light through the windshield.

Despite this, there is no need to panic.

Turn on your wipers. Slow down (gradually and safely). Use the road markings to help you stay in your lane. Keep a good distance between you and the car in front of you—like, more distance than you need. Breathe. Check your mirrors to keep an eye on the vehicles around you. Also, it's a good idea to keep both hands on the wheel.

The biggest thing to remember in any adverse weather condition is to keep calm. If you're freaking out, there's a higher chance you'll find yourself in trouble. You may react too quickly or not quickly enough and run off the road or out of your lane.

Also, slow down. We cannot stress this enough. If it's raining, snowing, sleeting, icing, or meatballs are falling from the sky,

SLOW DOWN. Going too fast can lead to an accident, and you definitely won't have enough time to react if something goes wrong.

Importance of Safety Equipment

Wearing a seat belt can double your chances of surviving a crash. It'll also more than double your chances of avoiding a serious injury.

Seat belts hold drivers and passengers in place and help the driver maintain control during a collision. When you wear a seat belt, you're less likely to hit the steering column, dashboard, or wind-shield. They also work to keep people from being ejected or flying around the vehicle.

When used properly, along with wearing a seat belt, airbags can seriously reduce death and severe injury during a crash. There's less chance that your head or upper body will knock into something inside your car. Remember, airbags are a supplemental safety device and should be used with seat belts.

Under Virginia law, the driver and all front-seat passengers must wear safety belts. If you're transporting anyone younger than 18, you—as the driver—must ensure that the passenger is properly secured in a safety belt, booster seat, or child safety seat. It doesn't matter where they sit. Passengers can also get tickets. If you get pulled over for speeding and the officer sees that your front passenger isn't buckled in, they can get a ticket.

Also, **according to Virginia law, any rear-facing child safety seats must be placed in the back seat of the vehicle. Children from birth to 24 months ride in rear-facing car seats.** They should be facing the back because if you find yourself getting rear-ended and your baby is in a front-facing seat, the impact could break their neck. How do you know if a child is ready to get out of a booster seat? Put them in the backseat of your vehicle. If their legs are bent over the seat, they don't have to be in a car or booster seat. Their feet don't have to touch the ground; just have to be bent over the edge of the seat. You should also make sure that the seatbelt isn't hitting them in the neck. Taking a child out of a booster seat too early could seriously injure them.

It is equally important to know that in the state of Virginia, it is illegal to transport children under the age of 16 in the bed of a pickup truck, even if it is equipped with a camper shell.

Proper Use and Maintenance of Safety Equipment

We all know the importance of wearing seatbelts and using airbags by now. Now, it's time to look at the best ways to use and maintain them.

Seatbelts should be worn low on your lap and against your thigh. The shoulder belt should be over your shoulder and across your chest. Never wear it behind your back or under your arm. They should be snug. If you're pregnant, you'll be safer if you wear your seatbelt buckled as low on the pelvis as possible.

With airbags, it's essential to **move your seat back to be at least 10 to 12 inches from the steering wheel.** Any front passengers should also ensure they aren't seated too close to the dashboard. Also, if your steering wheel is adjustable, tilt it down. It will point the airbag to your chest instead of your head and neck.

Your hand position on the steering wheel should be at 8 o'clock and 4 o'clock.

How do you check to see if your airbags are working? Well, it's definitely not setting them off - do not try to recreate any of the scenes from Seth Rogan's "Neighbors." You can check the airbag indicator light in your vehicle. Turn the ignition to the first position and hold it there. All the lights should turn on. When you turn the ignition back to the start position, the airbag indicator should blink and go out if there are no issues. If it stays on, you should get your airbags checked out.

Okay, we've given you a lot of information and statistics, but here is a story about how safety equipment saves lives.

One day, a woman was driving to work. It was like any other day—bright, sunny, and sure to be good. The woman stopped at an intersection and waited to make a left turn. The light came on, and she pulled out. Unfortunately, an oncoming car decided to run a red light and plowed into her.

The seatbelt constricted, and the airbag deployed. While her car was totaled, the woman was still alive and walked away with far less serious injuries than she could have had. While the seatbelt helped, without the airbag, she very well could have faced severe head trauma from hitting the steering wheel.

Without both, she could have shot through the windshield.

Put on your seatbelt and make sure your airbags are working.

To see how you're doing, be sure to take the online quiz for this chapter at www.blessedonlinedriversmanualcourse.com to see how you're doing. If you still need to set up your account, just email your name, email address, and the last six digits of your ISBN number to myclass@blesseddrivingschool.com. We'll have your account ready for you in no time.

CHAPTER 4
ROAD SIGNS AND SIGNALS MASTERY

I magine it's a nice day, and you're driving down a six-lane highway. You've got your space bubble around your car. You're not speeding. All is well as you bop along to the tunes on Spotify.

You come up to a sign. It's a bit weird-looking, but you're pretty sure you know what it means. It shows two lanes with one bending in -- the lane is ending. Onward, you drive, and once you reach the point where your lane ends, you keep driving forward.

Suddenly, there is a screech of tires behind you. Looking in your mirrors, you see a car swerving out of the way to avoid rear-ending you as you merge.

What went wrong?

First, when you see that sign, yes, it means your lane is ending. It also means you need to safely merge into the lane that isn't ending as soon as possible using your signals. Cars in the lane that isn't ending have the right-of-way. You are responsible for using signals and proper (SAFE) techniques to merge.

This is only one instance of drivers misunderstanding a road sign. However, by the time you finish this next chapter, you should be a pro at reading road signs and won't have issues passing that portion of the knowledge test.

EXPLANATION OF COMMON ROAD SIGNS AND SIGNALS.

We've already discussed what the various shapes and colors of road signs mean—learning that can help you in a pinch if you come across an unfamiliar sign. Now, let's take a deeper look at common road signs that you could see on the test or on the road.

Warning Signs

These signs give advance warning of hazards to allow drivers time to safely minimize risks:

 The right lane is ending and you need to merge into the left lane as soon as safely possible.

 The upcoming road is winding, which means there are a lot of curves.

 This sign signifies that a divided highway is beginning.

Watch out for merging from the right.

The road is slippery when wet.

A school zone and/or school crossing(if sign has double lines) is coming up.

You cannot pass other cars while on this stretch of road.

Road work is coming up, and you must take the noted detour.

Road work is coming up in 1,000 feet. **You should slow down** and be cautious.

Guide Signs

These signs help guide drivers to their destinations by showing different routes in advance.

Service & Recreational Information Signs

These signs let you know about any upcoming services and recreational facilities. Blue signs tend to indicate a service facility (gas station, hotel, rest stop, etc.), while brown signs typically show recreational or cultural stops (parks, zoos, etc.).

Stop & Regulatory Signs

These are signs that show you rules and regulations on the road and regulate the speed and movement of traffic.

 Come to a full and complete stop.

 No trucks are allowed on this road

 U-turns are not allowed, however you can make a left turn

 Left turns and U-turns are both not allowed.

 You must yield to other traffic and come to a complete stop if you cannot safely merge with the flow of traffic.

 A divided road is starting, so stay to the right.

The maximum speed you can legally travel on this road is 55 MPH.

 This is a one-way road, and you can only travel in the direction noted on the sign.

Let's take a look at another real-life scenario.

You're driving down the road and realize you've accidentally driven past the intersection where you needed to turn. Frustrated, you go to the next intersection and get into the left turn lane, intending to make a U-turn. However, when you look up, you see this sign.

You have only a few more seconds until the green light. What do you do? Go ahead and write it down.

If you wrote down make a U-turn anyway, then sorry, you would have failed. If you get to an intersection with this sign, you cannot make a U-turn. In this specific scenario, the only thing you can do now is make a left turn and find another way to turn around and get back to your previous route.

As mentioned, it is important to understand the different elements of traffic signs so that when you come up to one you may not recognize, you can still safely determine the meaning. If it's yellow, this usually means the sign is warning you of something. If it's white, the sign shows a rule (i.e. speed limit, no passing, etc). If it's blue, it's telling you about upcoming gas stations, hotels, or restaurants. Brown signs denote upcoming tourist spots. If the sign is red - stop. Also, orange signs mean there is construction.

Additionally, if you see an octagon, it's usually a stop sign. Any signs that are diamond-shaped give you some kind of warning. School and school crossing signs are usually a pentagon, while most regulatory signs are rectangles.

Remember this as you take the road sign test, and you won't need to stress about memorizing every sign. When it comes to taking the knowledge test, it's not always about remembering the correct answers but being able to eliminate the incorrect ones.

ROAD SIGN QUIZZES AND PRACTICE

One of the best ways to help increase your recognition of road signs and their meanings is to quiz yourself on them. Once you've learned to distinguish between warning signs, regulatory signs, and informational signs, you'll also have most of the work done.

Making flashcards can help you with this. You can easily and quickly quiz yourself on the meanings of common signs, and they'll help you learn them at a glance.

While it may seem tedious, you must study signs as much as possible. That portion of the knowledge test must be passed with a score of 100%. If you don't know the sign at first glance, it's okay. Take a beat and look through the answers. Usually, you'll be able to wheedle out most of the incorrect answers to determine the correct one.

Once you hit the road as a driver, it is even more important to understand the signs around you. They just may save you from an accident.

ROAD SIGN SCENARIOS AND APPLICATION

Let's look at some actual road sign scenarios you could face in real life.

Let's say you're driving down a road in a mostly residential area. You see this sign on the right side

What does it mean? And more importantly, what do you do? Go ahead. Think about it and then write it down.

If you guessed that it means a school crossing is coming up and you should slow down and prepare to stop when children are crossing the road, then you would be correct. Another reminder that the speed limit is 25 MPH in a school zone unless it's posted differently.

Moving on to our next scenario.

You're driving down a rural highway. There aren't many other cars around you. Or signs, for that matter. But then you see this sign.

What do you do? What does it mean? Go ahead and write down your answer.

This is a deer crossing sign. If you see this sign, you should slow down and be alert for any deer that may attempt to cross the road. It doesn't necessarily signify a special spot where they cross - just that deer are common in the area, so you should be prepared in case they leap into the road in front of you.

Let's say you're driving on a multilane road like an interstate. You look up and see a line of lights over the lanes. The two left lanes have this light over them.

You know the drill. Write down what the light means.

If you put down what it means to not drive in that lane, you would be correct.

What do you do if the light is this color?

The correct answer would be to move out of that particular lane as soon as safely possible, as it's about to change to red.

Here's another story for you about confusing traffic signs.

One day, a woman was driving through a city, heading out to a bookstore. Just before she reaches the intersection where she will make a left turn into the store parking lot, she sees this sign.

She notes the sign and continues to get into the left turn lane. The light is green. Focusing solely on that green light, the woman starts to make the turn, only to slam on the brakes when a car continues through the intersection.

It is then that she remembers the sign from earlier: Left turn must yield on a green light.

See? Green doesn't always mean go.

Applying road sign knowledge while you're driving in the real world is not only necessary but can also save you from an accident that could seriously hurt you or someone else. If you see an orange sign, slow down and start scanning the road for any construction —specifically for any workers. If you see any yellow signs, you should also slow down and be more alert as well. These signs warn you about potential hazards on the road ahead.

If you see a white sign, you should most definitely heed its instructions. These signs are letting you know about regulations. For example, the speed limit, as in our previous example, is the amount of time you must yield when making a left turn on a green light.

To see how you're doing, be sure to take the online quiz for this chapter at www.blessedonlinedriversmanualcourse.com to see how you're doing. If you still need to set up your account, just email your name, email address, and the last six digits of your ISBN number to myclass@blesseddrivingschool.com. We'll have your account ready for you in no time.

CHAPTER 5
VEHICLE OPERATION AND CONTROL

Taking care of your car and understanding all its different functions and controls are as important as knowing how to drive it safely. Maintenance and controls are also likely to appear on the knowledge test.

Did you know many auto accidents resulting from injury can be traced back to an owner failing to follow a recommended maintenance schedule? That's right—getting your oil changed and checking your tires regularly is essential.

In 2021, there were 622 traffic fatalities in tire-related crashes, according to the National Highway and Traffic Safety Administration. It's super important to check your tire pressure, get them rotated, watch the tread, keep them balanced, and replace tires in a timely manner when they reach the end of their life cycle. It can save you from blowouts and other scary situations that can put you, your passengers, and other drivers on the road in danger.

INTRODUCTION TO VEHICLE CONTROLS AND FUNCTIONS

While you most likely know that vehicles come with essential controls like brakes and steering, it's important to know what they are, where they are, and what they do. So, let's do a quick rundown.

Hand Brake: This is often located in the middle console of most vehicles. It's also called an emergency brake. Essentially, it's there to make sure your vehicle doesn't move while it's parked. It's good to use this when you are parked on a hill or incline as a backup to make sure it doesn't go rolling into traffic while you're not in the car.

Ignition: Depending on the vehicle, this is located on or near the steering column. Newer vehicles often come with a push-to-start ignition, while others will have a key ignition. For push-to-start, you usually just push until the vehicle starts, though some require a longer push or two. With a key ignition, you simply insert the key and turn until the engine starts.

Dashboard instruments: These tell you essential information about your vehicle, such as the speed you're traveling (speedometer); how much gas is in your car (fuel gauge); the temperature gauge; warning lights for fuel, oil, engine, water, tire pressure, and more; and how many miles are on your vehicle (odometer). Hybrids and electric cars will also have readouts for battery level and how much power is being drawn from or charged to the battery.

Steering Wheel: This can vary depending on how old or new your vehicle is and what package you have. Most will have a lever or levers for your turn signals and windshield wipers. They will also have controls to turn on your headlights and honk your horn (typically pressing on the center of the steering wheel). Some vehicles will include cruise control and functions such as buttons to answer phone calls and volume control.

Most importantly, the steering wheel controls the direction you are driving in. Having both hands on the wheel in the correct positions is essential when driving. Picture your steering wheel as a clock with all the hours. Typically, you drive with your hands in the "8" and "4" positions.

Floor Controls: If you are driving an automatic transmission vehicle, you typically have two pedals - brake and accelerator. The brake is on the left, while the accelerator is on the right. The brake slows down or stops the car, while the accelerator makes it go or go faster. Always use your right foot for both pedals.

If you are driving a manual transmission vehicle, you'll have a third pedal, known as the clutch, to the left of the brake pedal. Its purpose is to help you shift gears. This pedal is usually used with the left foot.

Gear Shift Lever: In some vehicles, the gear shift lever is located on the steering column. In others, it's located in the console between the driver and front passenger seats. In an automatic car, this moves the car from park to reverse, neutral, and drive. In a manual, this shifts the vehicle from neutral to first, second, third, fourth, fifth, and reverse. (You'll need to use the clutch to shift gears.)

Console Controls: It's important to note that your console controls can vary depending on the vehicle, but there are basic controls you'll find in most. Typically, this is where you'll find the button for your hazard lights, heating and cooling controls, airbag deactivator, and radio and volume controls. This is also where you'll typically find the display screen for GPS and other infotainment functions.

Other Controls: Depending on the vehicle, you'll also find controls on the door for your windows, locks, and side mirrors. Some have controls to move your seats (others have levers under or on the side of the seats for these). You'll also typically find a lever to open your gas tank on the driver's side or to pop the hood and/or trunk.

Learning to use and understand your vehicle's controls takes time. For most, it's intuitive, but you may still need to review your vehicle's manual to understand everything. And, of course, it will take practice with some vehicles, especially if you're driving a manual transmission.

Story time.

There was once a teenage girl who found herself with a manual transmission car upon turning 16. It was not an automatic like she had practiced with. While daunting, she was determined to get it down so she could drive herself places rather than relying on her parents or friends. So she practiced with her dad and grandfather on the gravel country roads around her house. She then reached the moment when she thought she was ready to take her car into town.

Things went smoothly for the most part, though she was still a bit shaky when shifting gears. She made it to her first destination without issue. Trouble struck when she went to make a left turn into the parking lot of her mother's office at her second destination. Shifting was dicey for her, and the added pressure of trying to make it into the parking lot between cars was even more anxiety-inducing.

In short - it was a disaster.

She ended up creating one of the few traffic jams her small town had ever seen, somehow blocking all three lanes as she struggled to shift and keep her car moving. Eventually, she had to get out and let a good samaritan pull her car into the parking lot for her as she cried in embarrassment.

Needless to say, it took her a long time to learn to drive a manual, though she never fully mastered it. Her next car was most definitely an automatic.

The best way to become familiar with your vehicle controls is to read the manual and practice. If practicing involves driving, make sure you are somewhere void of other cars (like an empty parking lot or a quiet street).

For most controls, you can sit in your parked car to figure it out. If you aren't sure about what a certain control does, READ YOUR VEHICLE MANUAL BEFORE YOU START PRESSING BUTTONS. You want to avoid accidentally turning something on or off and not know how to reverse it.

VEHICLE HANDLING AND MANEUVERING

Now that we've gone over all the various buttons, levers, and other controls your vehicle can have, it's time to look out how to handle and maneuver in your vehicle. We're going to go over a few essential maneuvers you'll face when driving.

Parking

There are definitely a few rules regarding parking that you must remember for the test and in real life. First of all, when parking on a public road, you should move as far away from traffic as you can. When parking on a shoulder, pull over as far as possible.

If you're parking on a two-way street, always park on the right. If it's one-way, you can park on either side.

Now, let's talk about **parking with a curb.** You should park as close to a curb as you can—though try not to hop it. Do not park more than one foot away from it. Turn the front wheels of your vehicle to prevent it from rolling into the street and traffic. **If you're parking downhill, turn your front wheels right. If you're parking uphill, turn your front wheels left.**

If there's no curb, turn the front wheels so that if the vehicle rolls, the rear will roll away from traffic. **This means downhill - turn the front wheels right. Uphill - turn the front wheels right, too.**

Do not park in these areas:

- Beside another parked vehicle (double parking)
- On crosswalks or sidewalks
- In front of driveways
- Within areas where parking is prohibited by curbs painted yellow or "No Parking" signs
- In a parking space reserved for disabled persons (unless you have a visible permit)
- One the hard surface of a road if no curb is present
- **Within 15 feet of a fire hydrant**
- **Within 20 feet of an intersection**
- **Within 15 feet of the entrance to a fire, ambulance, or rescue squad station**
- **Within 500 feet of where fire trucks or equipment are stopped answering an alarm**
- **Within 50 feet of a railroad crossing**
- In a way that blocks or creates a hazard for other vehicles in a designated traffic lane

Let's practice this a bit. If you're parking on a hill, going up the hill, and there's a curb on your right, which way are you turning your wheels? What if you're going down the hill, and there's a curb on the right? Which way are you turning your wheels? What if you're parking downhill, and there's no curb? Up the hill, and there's no curb?

Write this down. **When parking on a hill, always turn your wheels to the right.**

Wait. Did you catch that?

What did we say about always? If you caught that, good for you. Here's the full statement with the exception.

When parking on a hill, always turn your wheels to the right, EXCEPT when parking uphill with a curb. Then, you turn to the left. What this does is if your car somehow comes out of park (this is why you should always use your parking brake), it'll hit the curb and that will stop it.

Stopping

While stopping seems pretty standard, there is definitely important information you need to know. It very well could be on the test. Plus, stopping is more than simply slamming your foot down on the brake. (That's a good way to get whiplash.)

There are certain situations in which you must always stop your vehicle. They are the following:

- At all stop signs, red traffic lights, and flashing red lights
- When entering a street or crossing over a sidewalk from a driveway, alley, building, or parking lot
- At railroad crossings with flashing lights
- When signaled by flaggers directing traffic

- For pedestrians attempting to cross the street at a crosswalk
- **At the direction of a police officer. If you don't obey a law enforcement officer's signal to stop and the officer pursues you and is killed as a direct result of the pursuit, you will be guilty of a Class 4 felony.**
- **At the scene of a crash in which you are involved**

Let's say you hit a parked car. What do you do?

You should leave a note with all your contact information. Now, this isn't a good time to leave your ex's info like their mother's maiden name, social security number, or anything else to get them in trouble, no matter how angry you are. It should be your information.

A popular answer to this question on the test is "sit and wait." Do not choose this. What are you sitting and waiting for? While others are passing the test at DMV, those who didn't read this book chose to sit and wait, will still be sitting there! If you see a question asking what to do if you hit a parked car, you should choose to leave your information.

When coming to a stop sign and the car in front of you keeps going, you should stop at the sign and only go when the way is clear.

A few chapters ago, we mentioned stopping around school buses. To refresh your memory, you should stop for school buses with flashing lights and an extended stop sign when you approach from any direction on a highway, private road or school driveway. Remain stopped until all kids have cleared out of the road and the bus moves again. You also must stop if the bus is loading or unloading and there are no lights or signs.

The only time you do not need to stop for a school bus is if you are traveling in the opposite direction on a roadway with a median or barrier dividing the road and the bus is on the opposite side of the barrier or median.

Three factors determine the distance it takes to come to a complete stop - perception time, reaction distance and braking distance. **Perception time** is the time it takes to recognize a hazard. **Reaction distance** is the distance your vehicle travels between the time you recognize a problem and when you apply the brakes. Lastly, the **braking distance** is the distance your car travels after you apply the brakes.

These three factors are affected by weather, visibility and your mental and physical condition. Braking distance is also affected by how fast your vehicle is traveling, the condition of the brakes and tires, and the pavement condition. Wet pavement can double your braking distance.

This is the average stopping distance on dry pavement based on speed:

- **25 MPH - 85 feet**
- **35 MPH - 135 feet**
- **45 MPH - 195 feet**
- **55 MPH - 265 feet**
- ****65 MPH - 344 feet**

** This has consistently been reported as being on the test, so definitely write it down.

Turning

To make a right turn, you should be in the lane closest to the curb. First, signal your intent to turn. You should do this at least three to four seconds—or 100 feet—ahead of the turn. Look to your left to check the intersection for pedestrians and traffic coming from the other direction. Then, brake smoothly before and during the turn.

If there is a traffic light or stop sign at the intersection, you must come to a complete stop before you turn. Also, turn into the closest lane to the curb unless pavement markings tell you otherwise. You can then change lanes if needed.

To make a left turn, be in the furthest left lane possible, turning into the leftmost lane on the intersection road. Of course, this is unless pavement markings tell you otherwise or there are multiple left turn lanes provided. If there is more than one left-turn lane, you should choose the lane that best serves your needs once you enter the intersecting road.

Like with right turns, **signal your intent to turn with your blinker at least three to four seconds or 100 feet before you turn.** Look in all directions and check the intersection for pedestrians and traffic coming from the opposite direction. Keep the front wheels pointed straight away until you are actually making the left turn.

We've mentioned this before, but we're going to really drive in the point. It is so important to use your turn signals. If other drivers can't see that you are planning to turn or change lanes, it could cause a serious accident. **You must give a proper turn signal before changing lanes, turning, or entering or exiting a highway.** It is required by law.

Using turn signals communicates what you plan to do with the drivers around you. Develop a good habit of using your turn signals, or even hand signals, if you're unable to use the ones in your vehicle - even if there are no other vehicles on the road.

We mentioned above when you should start signaling your turn. You should also be aware that drivers planning to turn into your lane may not know exactly where you will turn. They could also pull out in front of you, which is why you should always be alert. Also, be sure to turn the signal off after you've completed said turn if your vehicle doesn't do it automatically.

Let's review hand signals quickly. **If you are planning to make a left turn**, your left hand and arm must be extended straight out, like the first arrow below. **For a right turn**, your left hand and arm should be pointing upward (see the middle arrow). **To slow or stop**, your left hand and arm should be pointing downward (again, check out the far right arrow below).

Now, let's put this in a way that you'll remember.

Remember, it's your left hand out the window—not the right. If you use your right, you just might smack the person sitting in the passenger seat next to you. If you're turning left, stick your left hand straight out. If you are living a righteous life and you die today, where are you going? UP. (Hence your arm going up for turning right.) If you're bad, living a terrible life, and you don't STOP, if you die today, where are you going? DOWN. (Arm down for stop.)

And that's Blessed Driving School's method for learning hand signals.

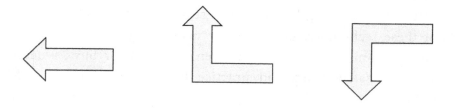

Mastering parking and turning is generally fairly easy. However, some maneuvers are more difficult than others, like parallel parking.

It is likely the bane of every new driver who plans to take the driving skills test, but it is important to know. Parking lots will not always be available, and you may find yourself having to park on a street. It was definitely one of the hardest maneuvers for our next example.

The driver in this story learned how to parallel park using buckets since her parents didn't have traffic cones on hand. They loaded them into the car and took our new driver to the parking lot of the local Walmart to practice. They would set them out at the right distance to signify cars and then guide the driver through the steps.

It was definitely a frustrating experience for all parties involved. There was also a lot of bumping into buckets, though thankfully, there was no damage to the car or the buckets. But it was all worth it after months of practice when the new driver passed her driving test and officially got her license.

Parallel parking was definitely on that test.

As with most things, the best way to master turning, parking, and stopping is to practice. As mentioned in our example above, use objects that won't damage your vehicle if you accidentally hit them to practice parallel parking rather than actual cars. Parking lots are also great places to practice many of these techniques. Large lots by malls or stores will usually have sections at the back that aren't crowded or busy, where you can safely learn and practice how to make turns and such.

Also, stay focused. Just because you don't get something on the first try doesn't mean you'll never get it. Sometimes, you need to do things over and over again before it finally sticks.

VEHICLE MAINTENANCE BASICS

Everyone knows that if you want to keep your engine purring and your car on the road, you have to take care of it. Neglecting basic vehicle maintenance can lead to getting stranded on the side of the road - at the very least - or an accident - at the very worst.

Here are some things you should check regularly on your vehicle to keep it in tip-top shape.

Check your tire pressure and get your tires rotated. This can help save you from getting a flat on the side of the road or from over-filling and having a blowout. A lot of times, if your tire pressure is only slightly low, you can get by with airing them up a bit. However, if you need to put in air often or the pressure drops too low, it could mean it's time to replace the tire. Rotating them makes for a smoother ride and can extend the life of your tires.

Once a month or before a long trip, you should check your tires for wear and damage. You can do this using the penny test. Take a penny and hold Abraham Lincoln's body between your thumb and forefinger. Select a point on your tire where the tread appears to be lowest and place Lincoln's head into one of the grooves. If the tread covers any part of his head, you're driving with a safe amount. If the tread is below that, your vehicle's ability to grip the road in adverse conditions is greatly reduced.

Check your motor oil and get it changed regularly. You should check your oil at least once a month. How often you change the oil depends on your vehicle and the type of oil you use. Regularly changing your oil will help reduce and remove any excess dirt that can build up in your engine. If you don't change your oil, it could lead to a buildup of sludge that will no longer remove the heat from the engine and cause an engine shutdown.

Check other important fluids like transmission fluid, coolant, brake fluid, and windshield wiper fluid. Transmission fluid is one of the more important fluids in your car - it lubricates and cools important parts of the transmission, which includes clutches, gears, and valves. If you have a newer car, it should be replaced every 100,000 miles. Coolant keeps your engine cool during the hot months and keeps it from freezing in the winter. It also prevents corrosion, foam, and deposits from forming. While you should check it often - especially before long trips - it should be tested every 50,000 miles. Brake fluid helps your brake pads slow your vehicle down. As the pads wear, the fluid goes down. If it falls below the minimum indicator, you should refill it and get your brakes checked. It's essential to replenish your windshield wiper fluid to keep your windshield squeaky clean. How often you check it depends on how much you use it - if you use it a lot, check it every time you get gas.

Test your headlights, taillights, and turn signals. We all know how important it is that you can see when you drive at night and that other drivers can see you and where you intend to turn or go. Also, you can get pulled over and receive a citation in Virginia if you are not using your headlights at night.

Check and replace your windshield wipers. If they are no longer cleaning off your windshield when needed or blurring up during rain or snow, it's probably time to get new ones. Being able to see in inclement weather (and in general) is incredibly important when driving.

Regularly check your engine air filter and replace it when needed. Having a clean air filter prevents dirt and dust particles from entering the engine and can help improve fuel efficiency and reduce environmental impact.

Check the cabin air filter regularly. Keeping this air filter clean keeps contaminants from entering the car. This can help with allergies and keep the inside of your vehicle smelling nice—as long as you also remember to toss out any McDonald's bags.

Test your battery regularly. This is important for many reasons. First of all, no one likes being stranded because of a dead battery. A battery test can help identify any problems before they become serious. It can also help extend the lifetime of your battery by identifying and addressing issues early.

Get your brakes inspected regularly. If your brakes aren't working correctly, they can lead to accidents and severe injury. Getting them checked often can help you find issues before they lead to severe crashes. Like with batteries, routine brake maintenance can help extend the life cycle of your brake system. This includes changing out brake pads and resurfacing or replacing rotors.

Check the belts and hoses. This is another thing that can help prevent even larger issues down the line. A belt or hose failure could cause an overheated engine, loss of power steering, or the loss of an electrical charging system. Serpentine belts should be replaced every five years or 50,000 miles, V belts every three years or 36,000 miles, and hoses every four years or 40,000 miles.

Trust us - it's important to keep your car in order. I learned the hard way that you should check your battery.

I bought a used car, but it was only about two years old and I had only had it for a few months at the time of this story. Because of this, I thought everything was in working order and hadn't kept up with regular maintenance. Early one morning, when I was leaving for work, I turned the ignition, and nothing happened. There was an odd noise but no indicator of what was wrong. After several frantic text messages, I discovered that it was likely the battery.

A friend showed up about 15 minutes later with cables and helped jump the car. I was able to make it to work, but was definitely worried about turning off the car. A couple of days later, the battery was changed, and all was well.

But I definitely learned a lot about batteries. For example, batteries typically only last about three years for a Kia Soul. Also, it's important to keep jumper cables in your vehicle and get your battery tested so you know to change it before it dies and leaves you stuck somewhere.

In Virginia, your vehicle must pass an annual safety inspection and display a valid safety inspection sticker. Your car must also pass an emissions test in certain parts of the country. Outside of that, it's good to check various parts of your vehicle regularly. It helps prevent accidents and ensures your car lasts as long as possible.

To see how you're doing, be sure to take the online quiz for this chapter at www.blessedonlinedriversmanualcourse.com to see how you're doing. If you still need to set up your account, just email your name, email address, and the last six digits of your ISBN number to myclass@blesseddrivingschool.com. We'll have your account ready for you in no time.

CHAPTER 6
TRAFFIC LAWS REVIEW AND PRACTICE

D id you know that police officers write an average of 112,000 driving citations a day? That's a lot of tickets. And you know what, a fair number of those drivers possibly didn't even realize they were breaking traffic law.

Being aware of your surroundings is important so you can experience all important traffic signs. It's also a good idea to have a basic understanding of all traffic laws. Because of that - and the fact that there will be questions on the knowledge test - we're going to review traffic laws.

REVIEW OF TRAFFIC LAWS

Recap of Laws and Regulations

We've been over a lot of traffic laws and regulations so far, so let's take a moment and go over them again from the beginning. This will help you to remember these better when you sit down to take your test.

Right-of-Way Concepts

As mentioned previously, **right-of-way is not a right or a privilege - it must be a given.** You must yield to traffic in specific situations to avoid accidents or tickets.

Yield also means to stop if you cannot merge safely into the flow of traffic.

Drivers entering an interstate from an entrance ramp must yield the right-of-way to traffic already on the highway. Other drivers may pull into the left lane to let you safely merge, but it's not their obligation. Drivers entering any intersection or traffic circle must also yield to traffic already in it.

All traffic must stop for a school bus with flashing red lights and an extended stop sign UNLESS the vehicles are traveling on the opposite side of a highway with a physical barrier or unpaved median area. Even if the signals are not working, if the bus is loading or unloading children, you must stop. **Only move when the bus moves and the way is clear**.

Be on the lookout for emergency vehicles. If you see flashing lights, you must take specific actions. **First of all, never follow an emergency vehicle closer than 500 feet when its lights are flashing.**

If police, fire, or rescue vehicles approach you from behind using a siren, flashing lights, or both, you must immediately yield the right-of-way. Safely pull over to the right edge of the road and stop until the emergency vehicle has passed. If you're on the interstate and an ambulance comes from the opposite side of the road and there's a barrier or median, you can keep going. If there's not, safely pull over to the right and remain stopped until they pass.

You must yield to funeral processions. Don't cut through. Don't join them because you are running late to work and want an escort through some traffic lights. Don't interfere. You'll be able to know who is in the procession as they will be driving slowly and usually have their hazard lights on. Also, unless there is a police escort, the lead car in a procession must follow all traffic laws.

Don't mess with military convoys. Always yield and never cut through or join. Military vehicles are made of steel; if there is an accident, they will crush you.

You must yield to pedestrians who are crossing a street within a clearly marked crosswalk or at an unmarked intersection. Also, if you are entering a street from a private road or driveway, you must stop and yield to all traffic and pedestrians.

Pavement Markings

Solid yellow center lines indicate two-way traffic with no passing allowed. You must always stay to the RIGHT of the line. **Crossing double yellow lines is permitted when you are making a left turn.** If you see broken yellow lines, passing is permitted in either direction. You should pass only when the way ahead is clear. Also, you should not speed while passing.

Now, if you have a yellow line that is broken on one side and solid on the other, **passing is permitted on the broken line side.** If you're on the solid side - don't pass.

White lines separate lanes of traffic going in the same direction and indicate one-way traffic. If you see broken white lines, drivers may cross them with caution. Solid white lines designate turn lanes and prevent lane changes near intersections.

Arrows indicate which turns may be made from the lane. If you see a curved arrow and the word "only," this means you can only turn in the direction the arrow indicates. If you see a curved and straight arrow, this means you can either turn in the direction of the arrow or keep going straight.

Stop lines, crosswalks, and parking spaces are also marked by white lines. Solid white lines mark the right edge of the pavement.

Speed Limits

A speed limit is the maximum legal speed at which you can travel on a road under ideal conditions—ideal conditions are super important to remember. You can drive slower than the posted speed, but it is illegal to drive faster. By law, you must drive slower if conditions make the posted speed unsafe. For example, you don't want to keep going 70 on the interstate if it's pouring rain or there's road construction. Slow down.

These are the maximum speed limits for passenger vehicles and motorcycles unless posted otherwise:

- **Interstate Highways in Certain Rural Areas: 70 MPH**
- **Non-rural Interstate Highways, Public Roads Not Part of the Interstate System: 55 MPH**
- **Rural Rustic Roads: 35 MPH**
- **School, Business, and Residential Zones: 25 MPH**

* You are required to travel 25 MPH in a school zone only when indicated by a sign or signal. Otherwise, maintain the posted speed.

Drinking and Driving

Legally, drivers 21 or older are considered to be driving under the influence (DUI) if their blood alcohol content (BAC) is .08 percent or higher. If your driving is impaired, you can be

convicted of driving under the influence with a BAC lower than .08 percent. Additionally, if under the age of 21, you can be convicted of illegal consumption of alcohol if your BAC is at least .02 percent but less than .08 percent.

Refuse to take a breath test or have a BAC of .08 percent or higher while driving, you can be charged with a DUI.

Insurance Regulations

To register a vehicle and obtain a driver's license, **you must have liability insurance or pay the $500 uninsured motor vehicle fee.** When you get a car, you must insure it with a company authorized to do business in Virginia. There are also some minimum requirements for liability insurance:

- **$30,000 for injury or death of one person**
- **$60,000 for injury or death of two or more people**
- **$20,000 for property damage.**

Headlights

Virginia law requires that you use headlights when visibility is reduced to 500 feet in inclement weather, such as rain, fog, snow, or sleet. Also, you have to use your headlights when you use your windshield wipers as a result of bad weather.

At sunset, turn on your headlights as soon as the light begins to fade to make your vehicle more visible to others. Headlights must be used from sunset to sunrise.

Lane Changes & Passing

Whether changing lanes, passing, entering, or exiting a highway, always use your turn signals and check traffic to the rear and sides.

There are times when passing is unlawful and unsafe:

- On hills, curves, at intersections or railroad crossings, except on roads with two or more lanes of traffic moving in the same direction
- Off the pavement or shoulder of the road
- When a school bus is stopped to load or unload passengers on a public road (unless a physical barrier or unpaved median separates traffic going in either direction) or on a private road
- When a solid line marks the left side of your lane

Safety Equipment

Under Virginia law, the driver and all front-seat passengers must wear safety belts. Also, if you're transporting anyone younger than 18, you—as the driver—must ensure that the passenger is properly secured in a safety belt, booster seat, or child safety seat, regardless of where they sit.

Also, **according to Virginia law, any rear-facing child safety seats must be placed in the back seat of the vehicle. Children from birth to 24 months ride in rear-facing car seats.**

It is equally important to know that in the state of Virginia, it is illegal to transport children under the age of 16 in the bed of a pickup truck, even if it is equipped with a camper shell.

Parking & Stopping

DO NOT PARK IN THE FOLLOWING:

- Beside another parked vehicle (double parking)
- On crosswalks or sidewalks
- In front of driveways

- Within areas where parking is prohibited by curbs painted yellow or "No Parking" signs
- In a parking space reserved for disabled persons (unless you have a visible permit)
- One the hard surface of a road if no curb is present
- **Within 15 feet of a fire hydrant**
- **Within 20 feet of an intersection**
- **Within 15 feet of the entrance to a fire, ambulance, or rescue squad station**
- **Within 500 feet of where fire trucks or equipment are stopped answering an alarm**
- **Within 50 feet of a railroad crossing**
- In a way that blocks or creates a hazard for other vehicles in a designated traffic lane

There are certain situations in which you must always stop your vehicle. They are the following:

- At all stop signs, red traffic lights, and flashing red lights
- When entering a street or crossing over a sidewalk from a driveway, alley, building, or parking lot
- At railroad crossings with flashing lights
- When signaled by flaggers directing traffic
- For pedestrians attempting to cross the street at a crosswalk
- **At the direction of a police officer. If you don't obey a law enforcement officer's signal to stop and the officer pursues you and is killed as a direct result of the pursuit, you will be guilty of a Class 4 felony.**
- **At the scene of a crash in which you are involved**

When coming to a stop sign and the car in front of you keeps going, you should stop at the sign and only go when the way is clear.

Let us give you a quote to think about.

"Ignorance of the law is no excuse."

This is a legal concept that means just because you don't know the law doesn't mean you can't be held accountable. A person who is ignorant of traffic laws will still be punished for breaking them. It's best to learn them in the first place so you can avoid the consequences.

Be sure to spend time reviewing the regulations in this book to become more familiar with them. A basic understanding of traffic regulations is important to pass the knowledge test and help you when you hit the road.

Traffic Laws Quizzes and Exercises

As mentioned before, this course and book are here to help you pass the knowledge test. We also have some suggestions for other resources you can use to help you really cement those traffic laws in your head.

First of all, try out this study guide and practice exam on the Virginia DMV's website. You can go through it to see how you're faring and what areas you need to work on as you continue through the book.

You don't have to take our word for it. The mother of a past student once contacted us to brag about her daughter a bit. She said that as her daughter took the knowledge test, she would read a question and then hear our instructor's voice in her head telling her the answers. Needless to say, she passed the test on her first try and found it easy to recall the information she had learned.

This book and its contents are based on the information we share in our classes. Read it, study it, and take notes. Do all this, and you, too, might pass the knowledge test and get your driver's permit.

Real-World Application of Traffic Laws

We've mentioned it before, but as you are taking the test, it helps to visualize yourself in the driver's seat to figure out the answer. Let's practice this a bit by putting you in some real-world scenarios. You could find some of these on the test.

Scenario #1

It's a nice, sunny day. You're driving to the store to pick up groceries for the week. As you drive through your neighborhood, you come up to an intersection with a four-way stop. Unfortunately, you're not the only one there. Two other cars have stopped at the intersection at the exact same time.

You are in the green car at the bottom. Who goes first? The red(right), green(bottom), or purple(left) car?

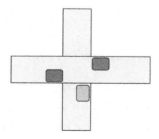

If you said the red(right) car, you would be correct. Remember our saying? **Left goes last.** If you are on the left or turning left, you go last. The person with no one on their right goes first.

Scenario #2

Let's say you're driving down the interstate on a cloudy day. You're going the speed limit, which is 70 MPH, and staying in the right lane unless you need to pass a vehicle going slower.

Suddenly, it starts raining. At first, it's just a gentle shower, but then it's pouring. You turn on your wipers and flip your headlights on, but keep going at the same speed. Behind you, you notice flashing lights. Slowing down, you eventually pull over. Why were you pulled over? Go ahead and write it down.

If you said for speeding, that is correct. Speed limits are the maximum speed you can drive in ideal conditions. Rain is not an ideal condition, so you should slow down.

Scenario #3

You're driving down a highway with a large stretch of grass separating your side from the other side. As you're driving, you see an ambulance coming toward you in the opposite lane. The lights are flashing and the siren is on.

What do you do?

If you said keep driving, then you're right.

Yes, you must always pull over to the side and stop when an emergency vehicle is coming, UNLESS you are on the opposite side of the road and there is a median or barrier separating you from the emergency vehicle. In that case, you can keep driving as normal.

Scenario #4

You are driving down a highway, following the speed limit and the flow of traffic. As you're driving, you look up and see this sign.

What do you do? Here, we'll give you some options.

    A. Keep driving and merge later when the road ends.
    B. Safely merge into the left lane as soon as you can.
    C. Nothing. Keep driving straight. The other cars will let you in.

If you said B, you would be correct. This sign means that the right lane is ending, and you need to merge into the left lane before the lane ends when it is safe to do so. You shouldn't wait until the lane ends to move over, nor should you expect that drivers in the left lane will automatically allow you to change lanes. All those rules about merging apply.

Here is another true story for you.

A driver is taking the on-ramp to the interstate. She speeds up and checks her mirrors and blind spots for other vehicles. There is a car coming up behind her. The driver has two choices. She can speed up - going over the speed limit - to get onto the interstate in front of the incoming car. Or, she can slow down and merge after the car has passed.

The driver decides not to speed. She keeps driving and slows down slightly to let the car pass and then safely merges onto the interstate behind it.

While most people might have sped up, the correct response in this situation is to yield the right-of-way to cars already on the road. You should slow down and merge safely without surpassing the speed limit.

Remember this when passing, too. You should not speed to pass another vehicle. You could get pulled over and receive a citation for speeding.

To see how you're doing, be sure to take the online quiz for this chapter at www.blessedonlinedriversmanualcourse.com to see how you're doing. If you still need to set up your account, just email your name, email address, and the last six digits of your ISBN number to myclass@blesseddrivingschool.com. We'll have your account ready for you in no time.

CHAPTER 7
DRIVING IN SPECIAL CONDITIONS

I magine you're driving down a road, and rain is pouring down all around you.

What should you be doing? What adjustments should you make to your driving? Do you do anything at all?

Of course, you do.

First, turn on your wipers and headlights. Next, slow down and increase the distance between your vehicle and those around you. You should not follow too closely since it takes longer to slow down and stop when it's raining or the road is slippery.

You should also be more alert and scan for potential hazards. Keep an eye on the car's tail lights in front of you and watch those passing cars. And be prepared for any sudden stops.

In short, driving in inclement weather requires an immediate adjustment. Let's dive into this.

DRIVING IN INCLEMENT WEATHER

Tips for Driving in Rain, Snow, and Fog

In a previous chapter, we've looked at driving in inclement weather, but let's get into it a bit more. The type of bad weather you may have to drive in varies from location to location, but you'll find that you'll use many of the same techniques in different situations.

First of all, let's look at rain. You must be more alert to the vehicles around you. Those in blind spot areas are much more difficult to see. It's essential to turn on your low beams not only so you can see the road better but also so that others can more easily see you. As mentioned in a previous chapter, you should also turn on your wipers if it's drizzling, but avoid it if it's sprinkling. Turning on your wipers for sprinkles could make visibility more problematic as it may smear up your windshield.

Remember - the roads are always the slickest in the first half hour of rain. This is because the water mixes with the oil already on the road. You also should avoid any standing water on a roadway as this could cause you to hydroplane.

When driving in snow, it's essential to clear off your vehicle before you leave your home. This way, you won't accidentally cause other drivers to crash because of snow or ice flying off your car. If it starts snowing while you're already on the road, it's essential to turn on your low beams and slow down. If you live in an area prone to a lot of snow, outfitting your car with all-weather tires or snow chains might be a good idea. This can help keep you from skidding and reduce your stopping distance.

Stopping on snow or ice requires a bit of finesse. You can't just press on the brake like you would any other day. This could lead to you skidding across the road and possibly getting into an accident. **Apply your brakes gently and gradually.** Give yourself more time and space to stop by taking your foot off the accelerator and letting the vehicle slow down before you lightly tap the brakes and slowly come to a complete stop or turn.

Let's say you're on the road, and a heavy fog suddenly rolls in. Once again - turn on your low beams. This is even more important in fog. Fog can reflect the light from your headlights back into your eyes, so you should use low beams instead of high beams. It would help if you also slowed down - as in every other adverse condition. Fog makes it harder to judge distances, so you need more time and space to slow down and stop. Also, be sure to use the pavement markings to help you stay on the road and inside your lane.

One of our instructors found themselves driving home from work one night after a fairly heavy snowfall. It was a bit unusual for their area, but they had driven on snow before, so they were confident it wouldn't be an issue.

The driver came up to a hill they needed to go down to get to their house. It was covered in a few inches of snow. While the driver was a bit nervous, there wasn't any other way to get to their home, so they went down. Rather than keeping their foot on the brake, they gently tapped it as they coasted (this was before anti-lock brakes were standard). When the car started to skid to the left, they turned the steering wheel to the left. While their heart rate was ridiculously high, the driver made it to the bottom of the hill safely and without going off the road, thanks to keeping a calm head and following the proper technique for driving on snow.

Staying calm, while often easier said than done, is one of the best ways to get through bad weather. Also, avoid smashing your foot down on the brake pedal. That is a great way to lose control of your car.

Handling Strong Winds and Extreme Temperatures

Let's say there's no rain or snow or fog, but the wind is something fierce. Or it's the hottest or coldest day of the year. Driving in high winds or extreme temperatures can still be hazardous. Let's take a look.

If you're in a pick-up, SUV, RV, van, or bus, towing or hauling, or on a multi-lane road with other large vehicles, you should be extra cautious during high or gusty winds. Any tall or broad vehicle has more surface area for the wind to shove against, meaning it's easier for that vehicle to be pushed into another lane or off the road.

Maintenance on your vehicle comes into play here. It would be best to ensure that your tires are properly inflated to have the best traction before you hit the road. Also, like other inclement weather, if the wind picks up, you should slow down and give yourself more space between your vehicle and others. This is especially true around large trucks and semis. Keep a firm grip on your steering wheel to help maintain control. You can compensate by steering slightly against a consistent side wind, which will keep you in your lane. If you get blown off course by a strong gust, do not overcorrect.

Make steering corrections when you're driving from areas that are protected from the wind to open ones. This means you should be extra cautious when driving on bridges, overpasses, open straightaways, through underpasses, or between hills and tunnels. There is a higher chance of sudden, unexpected wind gusts. Be on the lookout for road debris, which is very likely in super windy conditions. You want to avoid creating a pileup by dodging a stick or trash.

Like with rain, snow, and fog, if windy conditions are too dangerous to drive in, pull over somewhere safe until conditions are better.

When it comes to driving in extreme temperatures, a lot of this is stepping up maintenance to avoid finding yourself stuck on the side of the road.

In the heat, be sure to check your tire pressure before driving. Warmer weather can rapidly increase tire pressure, and you don't want a blowout. You'll also want to check and flush your coolant if needed. This will help with both your air conditioning and keeping your engine nice and cool. If you're driving and you notice your engine temperature moving over the halfway mark, you can turn off your air conditioning and turn on your heat (unpleasant, we know, but bear with us) to rest your engine. You'll definitely want to pull over, if possible, to give it an even bigger break. Call roadside assistance if you see steam or smoke, and get away from the car if you see smoke. Do not add coolant or water until the car cools down.

It should be common knowledge not to leave children or animals in parked cars during high temperatures. The indoor temperature of a parked car can reach 110 degrees in as little as 10 minutes. Also, bring plenty of water on long trips to keep everyone hydrated.

What do you do in extremely cold weather? First, before you even leave, make sure that your car is warmed up. This isn't solely for your comfort but to ensure the engine and components are warmed and working. You can also take this time to clean off any ice or snow that may be on your car. If you have a garage, it's a good idea to park inside at night to protect your vehicle better.

During extremely cold weather, it's important not to let your gas level get too low. Keeping it at least half-full lowers the formation of condensation and extends engine run time in emergencies. Also, avoid using cruise control or your emergency brake when driving in icy conditions. If you live in an area prone to snow or ice, keeping a few supplies in your car, like extra windshield fluid, an ice scraper, and a bag of salt or kitty litter for traction, is a good idea.

While you may think that high winds are something only drivers in Chicago or Oklahoma have to worry about, you would be wrong. According to the National Weather Service, while high winds are most associated with severe thunderstorms, hurricanes, and nor'easters, they can also happen due to differences in air pressure. If there is a high wind warning or strong winds in the forecast, the best thing to do is to postpone your plans and not drive. However, we get that this is only sometimes possible.

One of our staffers who grew up in Oklahoma is well aware of what it's like driving in strong winds. (Rogers and Hammerstein didn't write about them sweeping down the plains for nothing.) It can feel like you're stuck in a wild round of bumper cars, except there are no bumper cars, and it's the wind pushing you around. Keeping a firm grip on the steering wheel and making minor, incremental adjustments to your steering can go a long way in keeping you in your lane and away from other vehicles. It's also a good idea to avoid passing semis unless you absolutely have to, and for all that is blustery, SLOW DOWN.

The best way to prepare for driving in extreme weather conditions is to check the forecast well before leaving. If it looks too dicey, consider changing your plans and staying in. If you can't, give yourself enough time to prep before hitting the road. Also, regular maintenance will go a long way in ensuring your vehicle is ready for any weather.

Emergency Procedures for Adverse Conditions

Skidding or hydroplaning is an unfortunate side effect of driving in rain, ice, or snow. While you can do your best to avoid finding yourself in that situation, sometimes it's unavoidable.

So, what do you do in the event that your car skids or hydroplanes?

The first step is to try not to panic. It seems obvious, but keeping a clear head in emergencies is very important. Going over what to do as often as you can BEFORE you ever find yourself skidding or hydroplaning is a good way to ensure that you don't panic.

Next, do not slam on the brakes. This might be your knee-jerk reaction, but resist it with everything in you. Instead, take your foot off the accelerator and let your vehicle slow down. If necessary, and your vehicle has anti-lock brakes, you can lightly tap them. This will help your tires regain traction.

Be sure to hold the steering wheel steady. Moving it too much in any direction can cause your car to lose more traction and spin out of control.

Last, while you may be tempted to completely stop once you've gotten control of your vehicle again, don't. If you need a moment, find a place to pull off the road to get yourself together safely, but don't stop in the middle of the street. This puts you at a higher risk of getting hit. Plus, other vehicles around you could also be dealing with skidding or hydroplaning.

Skidding can be scary - we're definitely right there with you. One of us here at Blessed Driving School found ourselves skidding on a snowy and icy road in our neighborhood this past winter. Even though it was on an empty residential street and over in about 20 seconds, it was still enough to have us slightly freaking out.

Thankfully, the driver was going slow—way slower than the 25 MPH speed limit—and didn't slam on the brakes. It helped that their vehicle was equipped with a slip indicator. When the car detects a loss of traction, it automatically applies the brakes to one or more wheels to help regain traction and control. Once the vehicle wasn't sliding anymore, the driver eased on the accelerator and made it down the road and to their destination.

What do you do if you find yourself stranded on the side of the road? Definitely call for help if you can. But here are some other tips for when you find yourself in an emergency.

Keep an emergency kit in your vehicle. This can include a first aid kit, seasonal protection (sunscreen in warm, sunny climes and extra blankets in winter), rainwear, a flashlight, extra batteries, a visibility kit so you can be seen easily by other vehicles and first responders, water, food, jumper cables, a phone charger, a tool kit, and a flat tire kit.

Get your vehicle as far off the road as possible. You do not want to be stuck in the middle of a street or highway, where you risk getting hit by other vehicles. Turn on your hazard lights. You want to be as visible as possible, whether to help roadside assistance or a tow truck find you or to keep others from accidentally hitting you.

Stay in your car if you are not in danger while in there. If you're simply waiting for a tow or for help, you are safest staying in your vehicle as long as it's off the road and out of the way.

If you're stranded in high temperatures, keep your windows slightly open. It would help if you also raised the hood to signal that you need help. Again - stay in your car. It's much better than attempting to find help and getting heat exhaustion. Also, keep hydrated.

Stay in your vehicle if you find yourself stranded or stalled in cold weather. (Repetitive, we know, but it's essential.) You'll get colder much faster if you go out looking for help. Plus, you don't want to exert yourself more than necessary. Turn on your hazard lights and do whatever you can to draw attention.

Also, don't leave your vehicle running for long periods with the windows rolled up to avoid asphyxiation. You'll want to make sure that the exhaust pipe is also clear.

To see how you're doing, be sure to take the online quiz for this chapter at www.blessedonlinedriversmanualcourse.com to see how you're doing. If you still need to set up your account, just email your name, email address, and the last six digits of your ISBN number to myclass@blesseddrivingschool.com. We'll have your account ready for you in no time.

CHAPTER 8
SHARING THE ROAD WITH OTHERS

I magine you're driving down a residential road. The sun is out, and it's warm. You have the window down as you sing along with Kirk Franklin on Spotify. You're not going too fast; you're just enjoying the drive.

You come up to an intersection with a yield sign. You have two options. You can keep bopping to the music and not slow down. It doesn't look like anyone is coming. The yield signs are more of a suggestion anyway, right?

Or, you can slow down and stop to ensure there is no cross traffic before you continue.

What should you do?

You would be correct if you chose to slow down—stop—and check the intersection before continuing through it. You'd also see the small car approaching from the right, thus avoiding a collision. Following yield signs is not just about being polite; it's about being safe.

When you understand and know the right-of-way, you're less likely to find yourself in an accident.

RIGHT OF WAY RULES AND RESPONSIBILITIES

Right of Way Principles and Common Scenarios

Trust us, by the time you finish this book, you will have the right-of-way down to an art. Practice makes perfect, so let's review a few more right-of-way scenarios and see how you do.

Let's say you come up to an intersection with a traffic light. You need to make a left turn, so you pull into the left turn lane. When you look up, there's no dedicated arrow, just a light.

What does this mean? If it's green, do you have the right-of-way? Take some time and write down your answer.

If you said yes, you have the right of way on green, then you would be wrong.

When there is no dedicated arrow light for the left turn lane, you must yield to oncoming traffic when it's green. This means you need to wait until the coast is clear before you turn left. Usually, you will see a sign that says, "Left turn yield on green." However, it's good to keep this rule fresh in your mind just in case there is no sign.

Now, let's say you've arrived at a four-way stop. The car across from you arrives at the same time. They don't have their turn signal on, meaning they are going straight, but you need to turn left. Who goes first?

If you answered the other car, then you would be right. Remember that saying we learned all the way at the beginning of the book?

Left is last. If you are on the left or making a left turn, then you must yield the right of way to the other vehicle or vehicles.

But what if four cars pull up to a four-way stop all at once, and no one is turning left? What do you do? How do you determine who goes first?

There is no exact set rule for this situation, so usually, the right-of-way is given to the most aggressive driver or whoever decides to go first. After that, you would follow the "left is last" rule—whoever is the farthest right goes next, and so forth.

In our next scenario, you're driving down the highway and suddenly see a pedestrian dash across the road. What do you do? Who has the right of way?

Technically, on highways with no traffic lights, intersections, or crosswalks, you, as the driver, have the right-of-way. However, you are also expected to try to avoid hitting the pedestrian if possible. It's not "open season" on pedestrians, so please don't hit them just because you have the right-of-way!

In fact, let's take a closer look at sharing the road with pedestrians.

Generally, there are three types of pedestrians that are most involved in crashes: children, the elderly, and adults under the influence of alcohol or other drugs. As such, there are certain areas where you should be more alert.

If you are in a school zone, residential area, or there is a playground, be on the lookout for small children who could be playing near or crossing the street. You should also look out for the elderly, who may have poor vision or hearing and may move more slowly.

When you are making a right or left turn, you should also look for pedestrians first. **They have the right-of-way and you must let them completely cross the street before you start your turn.**

Generally, wherever you're driving - though especially on city streets where there are sidewalks - you should be aware and alert for pedestrians at all times. Even if you might have the right-of-way, you should be prepared to stop should one cross in front of you.

Interacting with Other Road Users

Before we get into the specifics of interacting with other drivers and vehicles, let's review signals. Good communication with others on the road is key to avoiding collisions.

You should always use your turn signals when you are turning, merging, passing, or changing lanes. Other drivers cannot read your mind, so you need to let them know when you are planning to move into their lane (or out of it). As mentioned, **you should signal at least three or four seconds - roughly 100 feet - ahead of the turn.**

If you are on a bicycle or your turn signals aren't working, you should use hand signals to let others around you know what you are planning to do. Here's a review of those (see the diagram below for those that are more visual):

- **Left Turn - left hand and arm pointing straight out**
- **Right Turn - left hand and arm pointing upward**
- **Slow or Stop - left hand and arm pointing downward**

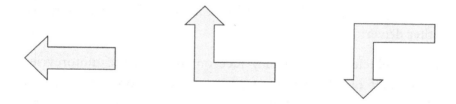

Unless you live in the middle of nowhere, you'll encounter other drivers and vehicles on the road. Understanding how to interact with and drive safely with them is essential. Let's review the different types of vehicles you will see on the road and how you should interact with them.

Bicycles are considered vehicles and have the same right-of-way as motor vehicles. They are also expected to obey the same traffic rules and regulations as vehicle drivers. It would be best to slow down when approaching bicyclists and give them plenty of room when you pass. You should also be ready to stop suddenly and look for them on public roads.

You should also note that operating a bicycle or electric power device (assistive mobility devices, toy vehicles) on any interstate highway is illegal.

Under Virginia law, a moped is a bicycle-like device with pedals and a motor. The motor can't be rated at more than two horsepower or allow the moped to travel more than 30 MPH. It's against the law to operate a moped faster than 35 MPH or on an interstate highway. You go over that, and it's considered a motorcycle, meaning you need to have special licensing and follow registration requirements.

Riders must be at least age 16, register the moped at DMV, and obey all rules of the road. They also need to carry some form of ID that includes their name, address, and date of birth. Additionally, they should be wearing a helmet. When you're on the road with a moped, be sure to give them the same care as any other driver.

Other vehicles that you may face on the road are motorcycles. About half of all fatal motorcycle crashes involve automobiles. They are often the result of the motorist's failure to see the motorcycle in traffic.

So, while it doesn't need to be said, we'll say it anyway—look out for motorcycles. **In more than half of all crashes involving motorcycles, the other driver didn't see the motorcycle until it was too late.** You're conditioned to look for four-wheeled vehicles on the road, meaning you don't always see anything smaller than that.

When driving around motorcycles, be sure to check your blind spots more carefully - since they are smaller than cars, they more easily slide into them. You should also check for motorcycles before pulling out, changing lanes, backing up, or proceeding through an intersection.

Never tailgate a motorcyclist - you should always give yourself plenty of time to slow down and stop. Give yourself an extra second to the following distance rule and double that in inclement weather. Anticipate their movements. While motorcycles are smaller, they will use up the entire lane as traffic situations and road conditions change.

Sharing the Road with Commercial Vehicles and No-Zone Areas

It's hard to miss them, but it's definitely important to know how to drive around semis and other commercial vehicles. Trucks, tractor-trailers, buses, and recreational vehicles (RVs) are longer, higher, and wider than other vehicles. They also accelerate slowly and require greater stopping and turning distances.

There are dangerous areas around these vehicles, and as a driver, you need to know where they are so you can stay out of them. These are called No-Zones. They're on the front, sides, and rear and are blind spots where your vehicle disappears from the other vehicle's view.

Side No-Zones: Trucks, tractor-trailers, buses and RVs have big No-Zones on the sides that are dangerous because they make wide turns. They are much larger than the blind spot for cars. If you can't see the driver's face in their side view mirror, they can't see you.

Rear No-Zones: There is a large No-Zone directly behind any large vehicle. The driver can't see you, and you definitely can't see what's going on with traffic in front of them. If they brake or stop suddenly, you have nowhere to go and could likely ram into the back of the truck. Always keep a safe following distance.

Front No-Zones: It's important to keep the front no-zone in mind when you are passing. You could get rear-ended by a semi if you cut in front of them too soon after passing or if you cut in front and suddenly stop or slow down. Semis take nearly twice the time and room to stop as cars. Trucks and trailers can be as long as 65 feet, taking you more than half a mile of clear road to pass. Be sure to check your rearview mirror for the entire front of the truck before you pull in front of it. Don't slow down; maintain your speed.

Wide Turns: Trucks, buses, and RVs often need to swing wide to make left or right turns safely. Note that they can't see you sitting behind them. **These vehicles' blind spots stretch up to 20 feet in front of the cab and approximately 200 feet behind them.** Whatever you do, do not try to squeeze in between a truck, bus, or RV and the curb or another vehicle.

I spend a decent amount of time driving on interstates and turn-pikes, where you are highly likely to encounter semis and other large vehicles. **If you find yourself in a No-Zone area, safely move out of that area without speeding.**

When approaching a semi driving slower than I am, I maintain my speed and change lanes after ensuring no other vehicles are in the lane or my blind spots. Usually, without speeding, I pass the semi. Finally, when I can see the front tires of the semi-truck touching the ground in my rearview mirror, I use my blinker and switch back into the right lane. I eventually pull far ahead, leaving the truck behind.

This is how you safely pass a semi-truck.

Tips for Safe Interactions with Commercial Drivers

Something to know about blind spots - when another vehicle passes into one, it's difficult to see it without turning your head from your path of travel. This is why they are the cause of a lot of crashes. Drivers will often change lanes, thinking the lane next to them is empty when it's not. Add in the fact that the other vehicle is too close to avoid a collision, and it's a perfect storm.

However, you should be aware of other vehicles in your blind spots and try to avoid ending up in other drivers' blind spots. We've gone over those zones for commercial vehicles. Don't follow too closely to any large trucks or buses. Not only can they not see you, but if they stop or brake suddenly, you won't have time or space to avoid a crash. Giving them ample space on the road helps you stay visible and gives you plenty of time to react to any sudden changes.

If you are passing a vehicle - be it a semi or other car - avoid matching its speed. Doing so can result in being stuck in a blind spot longer than necessary. Make sure that you can pass them quickly, safely, and legally before changing lanes.

Also, always use your turn signals when you plan to change lanes to let the vehicles behind you know what you are doing so they can act accordingly.

To see how you're doing, be sure to take the online quiz for this chapter at www.blessedonlinedriversmanualcourse.com to see how you're doing. If you still need to set up your account, just email your name, email address, and the last six digits of your ISBN number to myclass@blesseddrivingschool.com. We'll have your account ready for you in no time.

CHAPTER 9
EMERGENCY PROCEDURES AND PREPAREDNESS

E ven if you follow all the rules and protocols for safe driving, sometimes accidents happen. What do you do?

Let's imagine for a moment that you're driving along a rural highway with a passenger in the front seat. Everything is going fine. You're not speeding. There's not a lot of traffic.

All of a sudden, a deer dashes across the road. You're able to avoid the deer by hitting your brakes. Unfortunately, the car behind you doesn't have the same luck. They run into the back of your car because they do not have a safe following distance. The airbags go off, and both you and your passenger are wearing seat belts. However, your passenger is a bit disoriented and banged up.

What do you do in this situation?

If you're at a loss, don't worry. We'll walk you through the steps. Knowing this information could help save someone's life.

EMERGENCY RESPONSE BASICS

Overview of emergency response procedures

Let's go through what the Virginia DMV driver's manual says you should do if you are involved in an accident.

The first thing you should do is **stop at the scene** or as close as you can get without blocking traffic. Move your vehicle off the road immediately if you can. Secondary wrecks are a considerable risk if you or your car are in the roadway. You want to get out of the way quickly and safely.

Next, **be careful when exiting your car.** If possible, keep it between you and moving traffic. As mentioned above, secondary wrecks are a real threat, so you want to avoid them.

If someone is injured, offer them help if you can. It is essential to remember: Do not try to move an injured person from a wrecked vehicle unless you have the necessary medical training or there is an immediate danger. Don't try to be a hero - you're not Captain America. Unless the car is on fire or about to explode, or you're a doctor, nurse, medic, or EMT, do not try to get anyone out of a vehicle in a crash. Moving them could do more harm than good.

Report the crash to authorities ASAP. Dial #77 on your cell phone. If someone is injured, paramedics must arrive quickly to provide medical care. Also, any crash involving property damage, personal injury, or death must be reported to the police.

Exchange information with others involved in the accident. It's essential to have this information for your records and to use it for other notifications. You want to get the following information:

- Name, address, and driver's license number of other drivers
- License plate numbers of all cars involved
- Name and address of anyone injured
- Name and address of every witness
- Name, address, and insurance policy number of other vehicle owners

Lastly, you'll want to notify your insurance company. It doesn't matter whose fault it was; you must let them know. This will allow you to learn about any policy benefits that are available. It will also show compliance with your policy and provide you protection if the other party wants to seek compensation.

Something to note. Law enforcement is required to forward a written crash report to the DMV when an accident results in the injury or death of a person. They also must do this if property damage is over $1,500. This information will be put on the insurance record of every driver involved.

If you happen to hit a parked car or any other property and the owner isn't there, you do need to make an effort to find them. **We've mentioned this before, but if you cannot find the owner, you should leave a note on the car with your name, telephone number, the date and time of the crash, and a description of the damage.** Also, you need to report the accident to the police within 24 hours.

Let's go back to our story from the beginning of the chapter.

To refresh your memory, you've narrowly avoided hitting a deer, but the car behind you ended up ramming into your vehicle. The first thing you should do is pull off the road if it's possible. Once that's done, thank God for his protection, take stock of yourself and your passenger.

You're sore and have some bruising, but generally okay. Your passenger is the same. Check the road to make sure it's safe to exit the car. Once that's done, get out and check on the car behind you. You see that there is a driver with blood on their face. Talk to them and make sure they are conscious.

Keep them talking and dial #77. Give clear directions and instructions on where you are (or as clear as possible). If you can, help the other driver. Use a first aid kit that you should keep in your car. If not, stay with them and keep them talking until help arrives. Once the EMTs arrive, please step back and let them do their job. When police arrive, you'll want to speak to them about the accident and what happened. Be as detailed as you can. It's also important to stay calm throughout everything.

Now, staying calm is definitely easier said than done. Here are some tips that you can remember. First of all, slow down and breathe deeply. Observe the situation. Take a moment to assess what's happening around you before you move or do anything.

Focus on what needs to be done. Don't worry about your car or how much damage it has. Or that appointment that you're now going to be late for. Focus on getting yourself and any other injured people to safety and helping where you can.

Avoid reacting right away. You don't want to say anything that you might regret.

First aid essentials for drivers

Now that you know the steps you should take when you're in an accident, let's discuss first aid and, specifically, what to do if someone is injured in a car accident.

First, you should check yourself for any injuries. Can you move? Is anything broken, or are you bleeding? Address any of your injuries that you can first. Next, check to see if you should move somewhere safer to wait for authorities and para-medics to arrive. If that's in your car, then stay in your car. If that is a hazard, then you should move somewhere safer to wait and help other injured people to a safe spot as well—if you can.

As we said above, do not move a severely injured person. In fact, it's important to move any injured person as little as possible.

Keeping a first aid kit in your car is a good idea. You can use it to bandage up minor injuries and clean cuts. You should also use gloves or hand sanitizer in the kit to clean your hands before taking care of anyone to prevent infection.

If a person is bleeding, place pressure on the wound with a clean cloth or bandage. If they are unconscious, check to see if they are breathing, then check for a steady pulse. You can do this by placing two fingers on the inside of the wrist or the neck.

While you're waiting for help, keep the injured person talking. This can help them stay calm and conscious. You should also stay calm and speak to them slowly and clearly. This will go a long way to keeping them from going into shock.

If you have a first aid kit, here is how you can use it for minor injuries at a crash site.

Clean the injured area with antiseptic wipes for minor wounds and then blot it dry. Avoid using hydrogen peroxide or isopropyl alcohol, which can damage the tissue and delay healing. Once the wound is dry, apply antibiotic ointment and cover it with gauze or a bandage from the kit.

If there is a minor cut or scrape, first stop the bleeding. If it doesn't stop on its own, apply pressure with a clean cloth or gauze. Then, clean the wound, apply antibiotic ointment, and cover it with a bandage.

Let's go back to our scenario - the car rear-ending you after you avoided hitting a deer.

Let's say your passenger has a minor cut. Pull out your first aid kit. Use the antiseptic wipes to clean the wound. Once that's done, grab your ointment and gently put it on the cut. You can then grab a bandage to cover it.

With the driver in the other car, first, you need to assess if the head injury is severe or minor. If it's serious, grab some gauze and cover it to stop the bleeding. Keep it there until help arrives.

While having a first aid kit is essential, that's just the first step. You need to know how to use it should an emergency arise. It will only do you good if you know what to do. Here is what a first aid kit should have, according to the Red Cross, and the uses of those contents:

- Absorbent compress dressings - used to manage wounds that exude large amounts of fluid; used on abrasions, burns, or lacerations
- Adhesive bandages in various sizes - used on minor cuts, scrapes, burns, blisters, insect bites, and splinters
- Adhesive cloth tape - used to help keep gauze in place on a wound
- Antibiotic ointment packets - used to treat or prevent minor skin infections caused by cuts, scrapes, or burns
- Antiseptic wipes - used to clean and disinfect wounds
- Aspirin - used for pain management
- Emergency blanket - used to prevent or counter hypothermia

- Instant cold compress - used to reduce swelling and relieve discomfort
- Non-latex gloves
- Hydrocortisone ointment packets - used to treat minor skin irritations, itching, and rashes
- Gauze roll - used to cover closed wounds and burns
- Roller bandage - used to secure dressing in place
- Sterile gauze pads - used for general cleaning, dressings, prepping, packing and debriding wounds
- Oral thermometer - used to measure body temperature
- Triangular bandages - generally used with splints to support a fracture or broken bone
- Tweezers - used to remove glass, wood, or dirt from a wound
- Emergency first aid instructions

Preparation for roadside emergencies

While some accidents cannot be prevented, many others, including breakdowns, can. It takes being a responsible driver and a responsible vehicle owner.

Develop good driving habits. Knowing and following the rules of the road are good ways to avoid accidents. Following speed limits, maintaining a good distance between you and other cars, and scanning can help you avoid most wrecks.

It's also a good idea to avoid hard starts and stops since they can wear out essential parts of your vehicle. Avoid hitting potholes too hard so you won't damage your suspension or tires.

Keep up with a regular maintenance schedule. Check your oil monthly and get it changed according to the schedule suggested by the type of oil used and your engine (usually every 3,000 to 5,000 miles). Check other liquids often, such as windshield wiper fluid and coolant. It would be best if you also inspect your tires regularly. Ensure they have the right air (overinflated tires can lead to a flat). You'll also want to check the tread regularly to ensure it's not running too thin. This can lead to a higher chance of skidding on slippery or icy roads.

Get your vehicle serviced regularly. This will differ depending on your car, but you don't want to skip these appointments. Mechanics should examine your vehicle's crucial components, such as the engine, engine oil, steering, suspension, battery, brakes, tires, and lights. They'll inform you of any issues they find or if anything needs to be replaced so you won't find out the hard way —broken down on the side of the road.

Dealing with a breakdown can be scary, but it's not the end of the world. Let's say you have a flat tire. First of all, take a deep breath. Stay calm. Pull over and make sure you are completely off the road so you won't risk getting hit by another vehicle. Then, put on your hazard lights.

First, pull out the spare tire. Then, hitch up the car and proceed to change the tire. Make sure you fasten all the bolts tightly. You can then take the hitch down and put the damaged tire in the tire well. It would be best if you went to a mechanic as soon as possible to replace the spare.

If you don't want to change the tire yourself or don't have a spare, stay in the car and call roadside assistance.

There are several ways that you can prepare for the unexpected. As mentioned, having a first aid kit in your car is a good start. You can also keep jumper cables should your battery die. Keeping a spare tire and the tools needed to change it is a good idea. Also, keep a spare charger cord to ensure your phone has power if you are broken down and need to wait for help to arrive.

As always, good maintenance is the best way to prevent a breakdown in the first place, so create a schedule and stick to it.

ORGAN DONATION AND EMERGENCY RESPONSE

Understanding organ donation

When you eventually get a driver's license, part of the process is deciding if you want to be an organ donor. Regardless, it is something you should consider. While the number of patients waiting for organs changes daily, as of March 2024, the number of people on the national transplant list was more than 103,000, according to the Health Resources and Services Administration. Every 10 minutes, another person is added to the list.

You can sign up to be an organ donor at the DMV when you fill out the permit application. If you decide to be a donor, you should talk about this with your family so that if something happens to you, they are aware of your choice.

When you sign up to be an organ donor, you might one day help save someone's life. One donor can provide organs to up to eight people and can impact even more with tissue donation.

Let's walk through the donation process using our friend Bob.

First of all, Bob has to decide if he wants to be an organ donor. This can happen at any time whether or not Bob is getting a driver's license. Bob decides that he wants to be a donor.

The next step will hopefully happen a long time after Bob has made that decision, preferably after he has lived a long, happy, and full life. At some point, something happens, and Bob is in a life-or-death situation. The paramedics will arrive and start life-saving efforts, then transport Bob to the hospital. When they arrive, doctors and nurses will take up these life-saving efforts.

Once Bob has been stabilized, doctors will run tests to see how he's doing and how much damage is done. It is during this time that they will determine if Bob is brain dead. If he is, they will bring in a team from an organ procurement organization (OPA) to see if Bob is good to go with organ donation.

Once that's been determined, doctors and the OPO team will sit down and talk with Bob's family. They'll explain that it was Bob's wish to donate his organs and go through the process. They will then work together to help support Bob's family during this difficult time.

At this point, Bob's vitals, such as blood type, height, and weight, will be entered into the UNOS database along with the hospital's zip code. All of this is used to help find appropriate candidates. After the matches have been found, Bob will be taken to the operating room, where all of the organs and tissues to be donated will be removed. Bob will be treated with the utmost respect. Once removed, the organs and tissue will be taken to the transplant hospitals, where the candidates are ready and waiting.

After the donation, Bob is released to his family to follow whatever funeral traditions he wishes to have. A few weeks later, his family will receive a letter from the OPO letting them know which organs were transplanted. They won't know the names, but most OPOs will continue to support donor families with counseling and memorial events. It's also possible in some cases for donor families and transplant families to communicate.

We get it. Organ donation can seem scary and something you don't want to think about. Several myths exist that could discourage you or others from being an organ donor. Let's talk about them so you can make an informed decision.

The first myth is that there are more than enough organs for those who need them. We don't need to really get into this. As you've seen from the numbers listed above, there are not currently enough organs available. To drive the point, about 17 people die a day waiting for an organ transplant.

The next myth that you might have heard is that doctors don't work as hard to save organ donors. And it's incorrect. If you are admitted to a hospital for any reason, the nurses and doctors will make saving you their number one priority - even if you are an organ donor. Donations can only be considered once every attempt to save your life has been made. Then - and only then - will an organ transplant team be brought in. And they are a completely different team than the doctors and nurses treating you.

The next myth - brain death is the same as being in a coma, so you're not really dead. False. Brain death is a legal and medical definition of death. It means there has been a complete loss of brain function, and it can't be reversed. Typically, when a person is in a coma, there is still some brain function. Two separate doctors must administer specific tests to determine that someone is brain dead, and neither can be associated with the hospital's transplant team. So, trust them. If they say someone is brain dead, they're brain dead and not coming back.

Another common myth is that you can be too old for organ donation. In actuality, there is no age limit. There have been many successful organ transplants with donors who were over 50 - some of them were even well into their 80s. The medical condition at the time of death is more important than age.

Next myth - you can't have an open casket if you donate organs. This is also very much false. If you want to have an open casket after donating your organs, you can. Donating shouldn't interfere with any funeral plans, and the transplant team will treat a donor body with care and respect so there are no signs a donation even took place.

Yet another common myth is that rich or famous people get preference when it comes to donated organs. It's also very false. Status is not considered when it comes to deciding who gets donated organs. Priority is based on medical data showing a patient's need for a transplant and nothing more.

And to dispel a few other myths: no, your family does not pay for any of the costs associated with organ donation, and most religions also don't prohibit it. However, you can always check with your pastor, priest, or other religious leader about it.

Making informed decisions about organ donation

Okay, so let's say that you've decided that you want to be an organ donor. What do you do with that decision? You should register and talk to your family about it. It's not a light decision to make.

How can you register to be an organ donor? Well, one easy way is when you apply for a driver's license, learner's permit, or photo ID. During these processes, you will be asked if you want to be an organ donor. If you say yes, it will be noted on the front of your license or ID card. You can also sign up online through Donate Life Virginia.

Some things to know about being an organ donor:

- You must be at least 18 years old.
- If you are under 18, you must have your parent's or legal guardian's consent.

Also, it is essential that you talk about your decision with your family or a close friend. If something should happen to you, you want someone to know your wishes so they can make sure that they happen.

It is always devastating to lose a loved one to a car accident. However, being an organ donor can help create some light out of that situation. The family of Kristie Crowder, a cyclist who passed away after being hit by a car, was devastated by their loss. Even then, they tell people that Kristie lives on through the many people who received her donated organs, cornea, and tissue.

Altogether, she helped save or improve the lives of 58 people. Her heart went to a woman in Pennsylvania, while she also helped a man in North Carolina.

It's essential to decide on organ donation well before anything happens to you. It must be voluntary and altruistic. Plus, you must give informed consent and not feel pressured into it. This is why you should come to a decision on your own and then make sure you let the people closest to you know so that your wishes will be followed when you cannot speak for yourself.

Organ donation in emergencies

We touched on the organ donation process above, but let's look deeper into how emergency responders and doctors handle organ donation cases at accident sites.

As mentioned above, organ donation is only evaluated once all life-saving measures have been taken. The emergency responders that show up at an accident site will do everything they can, God willing, to save the lives of anyone injured and get them to a hospital as quickly as possible. EMTs do not have the authority to determine if someone is an organ donor. However, if the person has an organ donor card or bracelet or is noted on their ID, they can pass that information on to the hospital staff.

Once a person arrives at the hospital, life-saving efforts will continue. What happens after that varies, depending on the situation. Once the person is stable, they will then be evaluated to determine if they are brain dead. If they pass away during this time, doctors will move directly into assessing them for organ donation.

This is when the organ procurement organization team will come in to see if any of the organs or tissues can be donated. This obviously will vary depending on how the person died. Since we are mostly talking about car accident victims, doctors will look at what damage was done in the accident, as well as consider any conditions the person may have had prior to the accident.

Part of the OPO's job is to help assess donor potential and collect and convey accurate clinical information. They work directly with the decedent's family during the discussion about potential donation. The family will be kept informed every step of the way.

Additionally, you can rest assured that everyone involved in retrieving any organs or tissues to be donated will treat the donor with special care. It's an amazing gift that the person is giving, so of course, they don't take that lightly.

To see how you're doing, be sure to take the online quiz for this chapter at www.blessedonlinedriversmanualcourse.com to see how you're doing. If you still need to set up your account, just email your name, email address, and the last six digits of your ISBN number to myclass@blesseddrivingschool.com. We'll have your account ready for you in no time.

CHAPTER 10
FINAL PREPARATIONS AND TEST READINESS

I f you're reading this book and have already tried to pass the Virginia DMV knowledge test but have yet to be successful. Rather than giving up, you pulled yourself together and decided to give it another shot. The difference is, this time, you're taking more steps to ensure your success.

Henry Ford once said that failure is only the opportunity to begin again, this time more intelligently. If you've failed other times you've taken the test, the first step toward your eventual success is trying again. Nelson Mandela said that it always seems impossible until it's done. St. Mark 9:23 KJV says, "Jesus said unto him, If thou canst believe, all things are possible to him that believeth."

There may have been times when you thought passing this test was impossible, but we're here to tell you it's not. And we're going to make sure that you do find success.

Let's get into final prep before you sit down to take the knowledge test.

FINAL REVIEW AND PRACTICE

A comprehensive review of key topics covered in the book

We've covered a lot of material throughout this book - material from the DMV Driver's Manual, our courses on passing the knowledge test, and information from former students who have previously taken (and passed) the knowledge test. But let's quickly go over things you may see on the test one more time from each chapter. Be sure to compare what we have below with what you wrote in your notebook to see if something is missing from your notes.

Learner's Permit & Driver's License

- **Whenever you drive, you must carry a valid driver's license or permit.**
- **If you are under 18, you must hold a learner's permit for nine months before obtaining a driver's license. If you are 18 or older, you must hold a learner's permit for 60 days OR present a driver's license education certificate of completion to apply for a driver's license.**
- **You must be at least 15 years and six months old to get a learner's permit, complete a DL1M learner's permit and driver's license application form, and furnish proof of:**

  - Identification, such as a social security card, state ID, passport or birth certificate
  - A social security number (you can simply write this down, and the DMV will digitally confirm it)
  - Residency
  - Legal presence

- If the question includes the word "always" or "never," the answer is usually false. This is because there is almost always an exception to the rule.

Traffic Laws and Regulations

- Right-of-way is not a right or a privilege - it must be a given. You must yield to traffic in specific situations to avoid accidents or tickets.
- Yield also means to stop if you cannot merge safely into the flow of traffic.
- At a four-way stop, whoever arrives first goes first.
- If two or more vehicles arrive at a four-way stop at the same time, left is always last.
- Drivers entering an interstate from an entrance ramp must yield the right-of-way to traffic already on the highway.
- All traffic must stop for a school bus with flashing red lights and an extended stop sign UNLESS the vehicles are traveling on the opposite side of a highway with a physical barrier or unpaved median area.
- Only move when the bus moves and the way is clear (children out of the way).
- Never follow an emergency vehicle closer than 500 feet when its lights are flashing.
- You must yield to pedestrians who are crossing a street within a clearly marked crosswalk or at an unmarked intersection.
- Solid yellow center lines indicate two-way traffic with no passing allowed.

- Crossing double yellow lines is permitted when you are making a left turn.
- If you have a yellow line that is broken on one side and solid on the other, passing is permitted on the broken line side.
- White lines separate lanes of traffic going in the same direction. They also indicate one-way traffic.
- If you see broken white lines, it means drivers may cross them with caution. Solid white lines designate turn lanes and prevent lane changes near intersections.
- Arrows indicate which turns may be made from the lane.
- Stop lines, crosswalks, and parking spaces are also marked by white lines. Solid white lines mark the right edge of the pavement.
- These are the maximum speed limits for passenger vehicles and motorcycles unless posted otherwise:
- Interstate Highways in Certain Rural Areas: 70 MPH
- Non-rural Interstate Highways, Public Roads Not Part of the Interstate System: 55 MPH
- Rural Rustic Roads: 35 MPH
- School, Business, and Residential Zones: 25 MPH

* You are required to travel 25 MPH in a school zone only when indicated by a sign or signal. Otherwise, maintain the posted speed.

- **Colors on road signs have meanings.**

Red	Prohibitive or Stop
Blue	Motorist Services Signs
Green	Guide Information, such as Directions or Guidance Signs
Yellow	General Warning
Orange	Construction and Maintenance Work
White	Regulatory Signs
Pink	Hazardous Materials (HAZMAT)
Brown	Recreational and Cultural Interest
Fluorescent Optic Yellow	School Zones, School Crossings, and Pedestrian Crossings

- **Shapes of Signs have meanings.**

  o Octagon - stop signs
  o Triangle - yield signs
  o Diamond - warning
  o Pentagon - school and school crossings
  o Pennant - advance warning of no passing zone
  o Rectangle - regulatory or guided (vertical signs indicate the law while horizontal signs give directions or information)
  o Round - advance warning of railroad crossing
  o Crossbuck - railroad crossing (same as yield sign)

- **Types of Signs**

  o **Warning Signs:** These give advance warning of hazards to allow drivers time to minimize risks safely. Examples include winding roads, crosswalks, merging, lanes ending, roads that are slippery when wet, detours, and road work.

- **Guide Signs:** These guide drivers to their destination by identifying routes well in advance. Examples include letting you know upcoming exits, mile markers, upcoming intersections, which way to merge, and more.
- **Information Signs:** These inform drivers of motorist services and recreational facilities and include highway signs, rest stop notifications, upcoming restaurants and hotels, upcoming gas stations, and so on.
- **Regulatory Signs:** These regulate the speed and movement of traffic. They include one-way signs, stop signs, speed limit signs, yield signs, and so on.
- **No left turn signs also mean no U-turns. You can make a left turn on a no U-turn sign.**

Pre-Drive Tasks

- **Check around the outside of the vehicle for broken glass (windows, lights, etc), body damage, condition of tires, fluid leaks, direction of front tires, or debris on the ground that could interfere with movement.**
- **Check for small children or pets near the vehicle.**
- **Store personal items in the trunk of the vehicle.**

  - **Sliding books or book bags on seats when slowing or stopping will distract the driver.**
  - **Food or beverages also distract the driver from the driving tasks.**
  - **Valuables visible in the car may attract a thief.**

- **When parked at a curb:**

  - Approach vehicle from the front to monitor oncoming traffic.
  - Approach the driver's door with a key in hand.

- **When parked in parking lot:**

  - Approach vehicle from the rear to observe people or objects near the car.
  - Approach the driver's door with the key in hand.

- **Security:**

  - Check passengers for safe entry.
  - Lock doors.
  - Place the key in the appropriate location.

- **Driver's Seating Position:**

  - Adjust so driver's heel can pivot smoothly between foot pedals.
  - Adjust to allow at least 10 inches between the driver's chest and the steering wheel.
  - Adjust seat back for driver's visual needs.

- **Restraints:**

  - Safety belt positioned across chest and over pelvis (strong skeletal bones).
  - Sit at least 10 inches from the steering wheel and side airbags.
  - Head restraint - middle of the back of the skull.

- **Adjusting safety belt for proper fit**

  ○ Adjust the seat, place your lower back firmly against the seat and sit up straight (if equipped with adjustable center post mountings for shoulder belt height, adjust height setting so the belt does not rub against your neck)
  ○ grab the bracket above the latch plate and pull the belt across your pelvis (make sure it is not twisted)
  ○ push the latch into the buckle until you hear it click (check to make sure the latch is locked)
  ○ snug the lap belt by pulling down on the buckle end as you pull up on the shoulder belt

- **Sit straight but relaxed, and place your hands on the steering wheel. If your steering wheel were a clock, your hands should be at the 8 o'clock and 4 o'clock.**

Drunk Driving

- **Legally, drivers 21 or older are considered to be driving under the influence (DUI) if their blood alcohol content (BAC) is .08 percent or higher. If you are impaired, you can be convicted of driving under the influence with a BAC lower than .08 percent. If you're under the age of 21, you can be convicted of illegal consumption of alcohol if your BAC is at least .02 percent but less than .08 percent. There is zero tolerance. The only alcohol in your system should be mouthwash or medicine - no beer, wine, or liquor.**
- **12 ounces of beer (usually one can) is the same as a shot of liquor or a five-ounce glass of wine.**
- **It is important to know that the only thing that can get alcohol out of your system is <u>time</u>.**

- Just one alcoholic drink can affect your driving ability.
- Your chances of being in a crash are seven times greater if you drive after drinking than if you drive sober.
- Three out of every ten drivers are drunk between the hours of 10 p.m. and 2 a.m.
- You must have liability insurance or pay the $500 uninsured motor vehicle fee.
- When you get a car, you must insure it with a company authorized to do business in Virginia. There are also some minimum requirements for liability insurance:

  ○ $30,000 for injury or death of one person
  ○ $60,000 for injury or death of two or more people
  ○ $20,000 for property damage.

- If your license is suspended, your privilege to drive has been withdrawn temporarily. You may pay the required fees and reinstate your license at the end of the suspension period.
- Revocation means your privilege to drive has been terminated. In order to get it back, you have to apply for a new license and show proof of legal presence once the revocation period has ended.

Safe Driving Practices

- **Looking ahead** can help you spot risks early and give you more time to react. **Expert drivers try to focus their eyes 20 to 30 seconds ahead.**
- Search for clues on the road. Check for exhaust smoke, brake or back-up lights, and turned wheels on vehicles. This tells you that a car might be about to pull into your

path. Be aware of pedestrians or cyclists - they could potentially cross your path ahead as well.

- Watch for hidden intersections and driveways, curves, hills, and different road conditions.
- Check from left to right and then left again before entering an intersection.
- Look behind you. Use your rearview mirror to check the traffic behind you frequently, about every 10 seconds.
- The single biggest contributor to crashes is failing to identify a risk.
- At sunset, turn on your headlights as soon as the light begins to fade to make your vehicle more visible to others.
- You should use low beams when following within 200 feet of the vehicle ahead.
- If you're on highways, use your high beams unless another vehicle is within 500 feet.
- Use the two-, three- and four-second rule to determine if you are following far enough behind the vehicle ahead of you.
- At these posted speeds and on dry surfaces, this distance, in seconds, allows the driver to steer and brake out of problem areas:

  o 2 seconds Under 35 MPH
  o 3 seconds 36-45 MPH
  o 4 seconds 46-70 MPH

- You must change the following distance when the speed or road conditions change.

- Increase your following distance when driving:

  - behind a large vehicle that blocks your vision
  - in bad weather or heavy traffic
  - when exiting an expressway
  - behind a motorcycle
  - when being tailgated

- Whether changing lanes, passing, entering or exiting a highway, always use your turn signals and check traffic to the rear and sides.
- When passing another vehicle, you should check the traffic ahead, behind you and in your blind spot before you attempt to pass. Signal and then accelerate. You should then return to the right lane as soon as you can see the front of the passed vehicle in your rearview mirror. It is against the law to exceed the speed limit as you pass.
- When being passed, don't speed up. Maintain a steady speed or slow down.

- There are times when passing is unlawful and unsafe:

  - On hills, curves, at intersections, or railroad crossings, except on roads with two or more lanes of traffic moving in the same direction
  - Off the pavement or shoulder of the road
  - When a school bus is stopped to load or unload passengers on a public road (unless a physical barrier or unpaved median separates traffic going in either direction) or on a private road
  - When a solid line marks the left side of your lane.

- Here are tips for driving safely through a roundabout. As you come up to a roundabout, look for the street and direction signs. These will help you know what exit you need to take. They are generally posted along the roadside before you get to the roundabout. When you get to it, yield the right-of-way to pedestrians and bicyclists. You also need to yield to any vehicles already in the roundabout. The entry point will sometimes be controlled by a stop or yield sign or even a traffic signal. When the way is clear, you can enter.

- Don't change lanes or take an exit before checking for vehicles that may be continuing through the roundabout in the lane next to you or behind you.

- Most over-correction crashes are single-vehicle crashes and are usually preventable.

- An important note for driving through fog - it reflects light and can reflect your own headlights back into you. This is why you should use low-beam headlights in heavy fog and look for the road edge markings to guide you.

- Driving in heavy rain can be just as hazardous as driving in fog, especially if there's wind. It's especially difficult to see other vehicles behind you and in blind spot areas. Again, use your low-beam headlights. If it's a light rain or drizzle, turn on your windshield wipers to improve your visibility. If you turn them on while it's sprinkling, it could just smear the raindrops and make it harder to see. Make sure you have windshield wiper fluid in that case.

- When it snows, be sure to remove all of the snow and ice from your car before you start driving.

- Under Virginia law, the driver and all front-seat passengers must wear safety belts.
- According to Virginia law, any rear-facing child safety seats must be placed in the back seat of the vehicle. Children from birth to 24 months ride in rear-facing car seats.
- It is equally important to know that in the state of Virginia, it is illegal to transport children under the age of 16 in the bed of a pickup truck, even if it is equipped with a camper shell.
- With airbags, it's important to move your seat back to be at least 10 to 12 inches from the steering wheel.
- Your hand position on the steering wheel should be at 8 o'clock and 4 o'clock.
- Text messaging or reading of text messages while driving is illegal for all drivers. This is a primary offense - the first offense is a $125 fine, while it's $250 after that.
- The Driver Improvement Course can be taken once every two years for safety positive points. Usually those who got caught driving without a license or a seat belt ticket will have to take this class prior to obtaining a license.
- If you move, you are required to notify the DMV within 30 Days.
- If you're a new driver to Virginia, you must obtain a Virginia driver's license within 60 days of moving here.
- Title and register your vehicle and obtain Virginia license plates within 30 days of moving to Virginia.

Vehicle Operation and Control

- You should park as close to a curb as you can—though try not to hop it. Do not park more than one foot away from it. Turn the front wheels of your vehicle to prevent it from rolling into the street and traffic. **When parking on a hill, always turn your wheels to the right unless you are uphill with a curb. Then, turn your wheels to the left.**
- **If there's no curb,** turn the front wheels so that if the vehicle rolls, the rear will roll away from traffic. **This means downhill - turn the front wheels right. Uphill - turn the front wheels right, too.**

- **Do not park in these areas:**

  - Beside another parked vehicle (double parking)
  - On crosswalks or sidewalks
  - In front of driveways
  - Within areas where parking is prohibited by curbs painted yellow or "No Parking" signs
  - In a parking space reserved for disabled persons (unless you have a visible permit)
  - One the hard surface of a road if no curb is present
  - **Within 15 feet of a fire hydrant**
  - **Within 20 feet of an intersection**
  - **Within 15 feet of the entrance to a fire, ambulance or rescue squad station**
  - **Within 500 feet of where fire trucks or equipment are stopped answering an alarm**
  - **Within 50 feet of a railroad crossing**
  - In a way that blocks or creates a hazard for other vehicles in a designated traffic lane.

- **There are certain situations in which you must always stop your vehicle.** They are the following:

  - At all stop signs, red traffic lights, and flashing red lights
  - When entering a street or crossing over a sidewalk from a driveway, alley, building, or parking lot
  - At railroad crossings with flashing lights
  - When signaled by flaggers directing traffic
  - For pedestrians attempting to cross the street at a crosswalk
  - **At the direction of a police officer. If you don't obey a law enforcement officer's signal to stop and the officer pursues you and is killed as a direct result of the pursuit, you will be guilty of a Class 4 felony.**
  - **At the scene of a crash in which you are involved**

- **Perception time** is the time it takes to recognize a hazard.
- **Reaction distance** is the distance your vehicle travels between the time you recognize a problem and when you apply the brakes.
- **Braking distance** is the distance your car travels after you apply the brakes.
- **This is the average stopping distance on dry pavement based on speed:**

  - **25 MPH - 85 feet**
  - **35 MPH - 135 feet**
  - **45 MPH - 195 feet**
  - **55 MPH - 265 feet**
  - ****65 MPH - 344 feet**

** This has consistently been reported as being on the test, so definitely write it down.**

- **To make a right turn,** you should be in the lane closest to the curb. First, signal your intent to turn. You should do this at least three to four seconds—or 100 feet—ahead of the turn. Look to your left to check the intersection for pedestrians and traffic coming from the other direction. Then, brake smoothly before and during the turn.
- **To make a left turn,** be in the furthest left lane possible, turning into the leftmost lane on the intersection road. Of course, this is unless pavement markings tell you otherwise or there are multiple left turn lanes provided. If there is more than one left-turn lane, you should choose the lane that best serves your needs once you enter the intersecting road.
- **Keep front wheels pointed straight until actually making a left turn.**
- Like with right turns, **signal your intent to turn with your blinker at least three to four seconds or 100 feet before you turn.**
- **You must give a proper turn signal before changing lanes, turning, or entering or exiting a highway.**
- **Let's review hand signals quickly. If you are planning to make a left turn, your left hand and arm must be extended straight out. For a right turn, your left hand and arm should be pointing upward. To slow or stop, your left hand and arm should be pointing downward.**
- **Generally, there are three types of pedestrians that are most involved in crashes: children, the elderly, and adults under the influence of alcohol or other drugs.**
- **When you are making a right or left turn, you should also look for pedestrians first. They have the right-of-way and you must let them completely cross the street before you start your turn.**

- Bicycles are considered vehicles and have the same right-of-way as motor vehicles.
- Under Virginia law, a moped is a bicycle-like device with pedals and a motor. The motor can't be rated at more than two horsepower or allow the moped to travel more than 30 MPH. It's against the law to operate a moped faster than 35 MPH or on an interstate highway.
- Riders must be at least age 16 and obey all rules of the road. They also need to carry some form of ID that includes their name, address, and date of birth. Additionally, they should be wearing a helmet.
- In more than half of all crashes involving motorcycles, the other driver didn't see the motorcycle until it was too late.
- **Side No-Zones:** Trucks, tractor-trailers, buses and RVs have big No-Zones on the sides that are dangerous because they make wide turns. They are much larger than the blind spot for cars. If you can't see the driver's face in their side view mirror, they can't see you.
- **Rear No-Zones:** There is a large No-Zone directly behind any large vehicle. The driver can't see you, and you definitely can't see what's going on with traffic in front of them. If they brake or stop suddenly, you have nowhere to go and could potentially crash into the back. Always keep a safe following distance.
- **Front No-Zones:** It's important to keep the front no-zone in mind when you are passing. You could get rear-ended by a semi if you cut in front of them too soon after passing or if you cut in front and suddenly stop or slow down. The driver in the truck behind you would be forced to slam on their brakes - they take nearly twice the time and room to stop as cars. Trucks and trailers can be as long as 65 feet, taking you more than half a mile of clear road to pass. Be

sure to check your rearview mirror for the entire front of the truck before you pull in front of it. Don't slow down; maintain your speed.

- **Wide Turns:** Trucks, buses, and RVs often need to swing wide to make left or right turns safely. Note that they can't see you sitting behind them. **These vehicles' blind spots stretch up to 20 feet in front of the cab and approximately 200 feet behind them.** Whatever you do, do not try to squeeze in between a truck, bus, or RV and the curb or another vehicle.

Traditional Mirror Views and Blind Spots

- **The large blind zone areas and the overlap between the said and rear mirrors when using traditional mirror settings.**
- **Adjusting the side mirror setting 15 degrees outward allows you to see the lanes to the sides and does not overlap as much with the area you can already see in your rearview mirror.**

Vision Standards

- **Driver's License - Unrestricted**

  - **20/40 or better vision in one or both eyes**
  - 100 degrees or better horizontal vision in one or both eyes, or comparable measurement that shows a field of vision within this range.

- **Driving - Restricted to daylight hours only**

  o **20/70 or better vision in one or both eyes**
  o 70 degrees, or better, horizontal vision. If you have vision in only one eye, you must have horizontal vision of at least 30 degrees or better when looking toward your nose and 40 degrees or better when looking toward your temple or a comparable measurement that shows a field of vision within this range.
  o **A daylight driving-only restricted license permits you to drive only during the period of time beginning a half-hour after sunrise and ending a half-hour before sunset.**

Matt Biondi said this: "Persistence can change failure into extraordinary achievement." It doesn't matter if you've failed the test in the past. Or if this is your first time trying. The fact that you are putting in the work - persisting - will go a long way in passing the knowledge test.

Now that you're in the final steps before taking your test, it's best to identify areas on which you need to focus more. If you put more effort into those areas, everything else will fall into place.

A good way to do this is to develop a study strategy. Make a checklist of each lesson or concept that could be on the exam (we've helped you out with this) and go through each one. Mark it off your list when you feel confident you understand the important information.

Take a quick practice test before you start diving into full study sessions. This will help you identify the areas that will need more time and effort when it comes to studying. It will also help you to know the areas that you already have down. Not so you can skip them, but so you can know what to prioritize.

Practice tests and simulations

Taking practice exams is an essential part of preparing to take the Virginia DMV knowledge test. You can easily find full-length practice tests on the DMV website. These are important not only to test how much knowledge you have retained from our course but also to help you become familiar with it—how the questions are worded, the types of answers provided, how long it takes, etc.

Part of passing the test is being familiar with the format and what it feels like to have a time limit while taking it. The more familiar you are with the test, the more comfortable you'll be while taking it, and the more likely you will pass.

Like high school students take practice tests before the SAT or ACT, a practice test of the knowledge exam can help you get your best score.

Test anxiety is one of the top challenges to scoring what you need on tests. Like other people, Lisa struggled to pass tests in school because of this. It even affected her when it came time to take the knowledge test. However, knowing that she suffered from test anxiety helped her find a good study strategy. Part of that was taking practice tests. So, she would study the material and then stop to take a practice test to check how much of the information she retained and areas where she needed improvement.

When it came time to take the knowledge exam, Lisa found that her anxiety was low. Because she knew what to expect, she breezed through her knowledge exam and passed it on the first try.

You, too, could be like Lisa.

So, how can you best simulate the knowledge test? Most online sources where you can take the practice exam will already have a time limit. If they don't, be sure to set a timer on your phone or watch so you know what it feels like to be on a limit.

It's also essential to go over all the questions you got wrong. Carefully read the question and how it was worded, then read the answer and how it was worded. A lot of passing the test is about carefully reading the questions and instructions and then all your options. Remember what we said earlier about questions with "never" or "always"? These can trip you up as there is usually an exception to most rules.

Here's another good tip to remember as you take the test. Don't choose the first answer that pops into your head. Be sure to read all of the answers before choosing one. It could be A and B. It could be A, B, and C, but you missed those options because you immediately chose A and didn't read down to C.

Here's an illustration of how this works. Let's talk about turn signals. Sometimes, you see someone with the proper signal on and they go left. Sometimes, they have their left on, and they go right. Or maybe they have the music on. They're dancing and feeling the beat. Then, their leg comes up and hits the turn signal - they think it's just part of the beat. They're "turnt", but are they turning? Some of you might have thought, well, just because they have their turn signal all, they could have turned it on by mistake.

You just said the first thing that came to your mind. And you could do that on the test and get it wrong. You see the turn signal light, so that means turn. A turn signal could mean turning. It could also mean that someone has already made the turn and they forgot to turn it off. Or they turned it on by mistake. An active turn signal light simply means that someone may or may not turn.

Mental and emotional readiness

How do you ensure you are mentally and emotionally ready to take the knowledge exam? Well, the first thing to do is stop, take a breath, and relax. While we want you to pass on the first try just as much as you do, know that it's not the end of the world if you don't—part of what builds anxiety before a test is a strong desire to pass. Rather than let the fear of failure trip you up, channel it into your preparation so you can succeed.

If it helps, spend some time praying or meditating—whatever works for you. It can help ease your anxiety about tests and help you focus and concentrate during study sessions and when you sit down to take the test.

Be sure to allow yourself plenty of time to study and prepare before you take the test. While it never hurts to pray for divine help from God, you still need to put in the work and make sure that you're ready. The more you study, the more prepared you'll feel and the more focused you'll be during the exam.

James 2:14 says, "What doth it profit, my brethren, though a man says he hath faith, and have not works? Can faith save him?" We need faith and works.

As mentioned, test anxiety can affect anyone—even us here at Blessed Driving School. Em was an absolute wreck the first time she took the ACT in high school. She hadn't studied as much as required, and her heart pounded as she sat down for the exam. She fixated on the clock and the time remaining for each section rather than focusing on answering questions accurately. While her performance wasn't poor, it still fell short of achieving the desired score.

So, what did she do? She decided to retake the ACT, except this time, she scheduled it much later to allow herself ample time to study diligently. She then took the time to study for the test earnestly. She got a book complete with ACT practice tests and began taking them. While she was more familiar with the test format after taking it the first time, she wanted to be comfortable with it. So, practice tests became a regular part of her study routine, especially timed practice tests.

You can be confident that she felt more confident the next time she took the ACT. She was more prepared and knew what to expect. Her studying paid off—her score went up. She was happy with what she got and didn't need to retake the test. One thing that helped was when she went in to take the test a second time; she told herself she would do better this time. And then she did.

Positive thinking can tremendously reduce test anxiety and improve your performance. You should focus on studying and preparing and walk into the test facility believing you'll pass. If you go into the test thinking that you won't pass or do a good job, you just might manifest that. So be sure to stay positive.

God willing, you got this. We're sure.

CONCLUSION

There you have it. Everything you need to know to pass the Virginia DMV learner's permit test. We've passed on all our knowledge and wisdom to help you pass. By now, you should have a good grasp of the following:

- Understanding the Learner's Permit Test and Licensing Process
- Virginia Traffic Laws and Regulations
- Safe Driving Practices
- Road Signs and Signals
- Vehicle Operation and Control
- Driving in Special Conditions
- Sharing the Road with Others
- Emergency Procedures and Preparedness

It's not just about passing the test; it's about applying this knowledge to your daily life. This book equips you to be a confident, responsible, and safe driver. It's your key to building a solid foundation for good driving habits.

We, the team at Blessed Driving School, are truly grateful that you've chosen our course and our book to guide you on your journey to passing the learner's permit test and becoming a safe and responsible driver. We've done our part; now, it's your turn to take the wheel and drive the rest of the way.

May God bless You.

WORKS CITED

1. Virginia Department of Motor Vehicles, "Insurance Requirements, https://www.dmv.virginia.gov/vehicles/insurance-requirements
2. American Additions Centers, "Blood Alcohol Content Calculator," https://alcohol.org/bac-calculator/
3. Virginia Department of Motor Vehicles, "Virginia Driver's Manual." Dec. 1, 2023, https://www.dmv.virginia.gov/licenses-ids/exams/manual
4. CPR Educators, Inc. "Basic First Aid Guide for Common Injuries," https://cpreducatorsinc.com/basic-first-aid-guide-for-common-injuries/
5. American Red Cross, "Make a First Aid Kit," https://www.redcross.org/get-help/how-to-prepare-for-emergencies/anatomy-of-a-first-aid-kit.htm
6. University of Colorado Denver, "For Me, It's Test Anxiety," Oct. 7, 2022, https://www.ucdenver.edu/student/stories/library/stories-from-the-hub/test-anxiety1
7. Jiffy Lube, "Summertime Safe: What to Pack in Your Hot Weather Car Emergency Kit," https://www.jiffylubeontario.com/summertime-safe-what-to-pack-in-your-hot-weather-car-emergency-kit/
8. Zachary Hansen, "Arizona Extreme Heat: 7 Tips if Your Car Breaks Down on a Road Trip," *The Republic,* June 16, 2017, https://www.azcentral.com/story/travel/arizona/road-trips/2017/06/16/arizona-extreme-heat-weather-prevent-car-breakdown/397272001/
9. Cooney and Conway, "14 Tips for Driving in Extreme Winter Conditions," *CooneyConway.com,* https://www.cooneyconway.com/blog/14-tips-driving-extreme-winter-conditions
10. Allstate, "The Car Maintenance Checklist," *Allstate.com,* June 2023, https://www.allstate.com/resources/car-insurance/car-maintenance-tips

Made in the USA
Middletown, DE
04 October 2024

62029817R10089